# *Save Thousands on Your Property Taxes!*

# Save Thousands on Your Property Taxes!

Henry W. Willen, Ph.D.

*Edited by Richard Stockton*

Collier Books / Macmillan Publishing Company · *New York*

Maxwell Macmillan Canada · *Toronto*

Maxwell Macmillan International · *New York* · *Oxford* · *Singapore* · *Sydney*

Collier Books
Macmillan Publishing Company
866 Third Avenue, New York, NY 10022

Maxwell Macmillan Canada, Inc.
1200 Eglinton Avenue East, Suite 200
Don Mills, Ontario M3C 3Ni

Macmillan Publishing Company is part of the Maxwell Communication Group of Companies.

Library of Congress Cataloging-in-Publication Data
Willen, Henry W.
  Save thousands on your property taxes! / Henry W. Willen : edited by Richard Stockton.
    p.   cm.
  Includes bibliographical references and index.
  ISBN 0-02-038315-0
  1. Real property tax—Law and legislation—United States.   2. Tax
protests and appeals—United States.   3. Tax assessment—Law and
legislation—United States.   I. Stockton, Richard B.   II. Title.
KF6760.W55   1991
343.7305′4—dc20
[347.30354]          91-27123          CIP

Macmillan books are available at special discounts for bulk purchases for sales promotions, premiums, fund-raising, or educational use. For details, contact:

  Special Sales Director
  Macmillan Publishing Company
  866 Third Avenue
  New York, NY 10022

First Collier Books Edition 1991

10   9   8   7   6   5   4   3   2   1

Designed by Nancy Sugihara

Printed in the United States of America

*To my parents, who taught me to cope with "the slings and arrows of outrageous fortune" (the warp and woof of most lives) by virtue of humor, patience, and self-reliance.*

*Thanks to the computer expertise of Nicholas Masters, Esq., Renee Stolpen and Larry LaRoche, the advice of Bernard Bastacky, and many others, this endeavor has been one of the most enjoyable of my life.*

# Contents

# *Preface*

This publication is designed to provide accurate and authoritative information to homeowners in regard to the subject matter; see an attorney before acting as a consultant. It is sold with the understanding that the publisher is not engaged in rendering legal, accounting, or other professional services. If legal or other professional assistance is required, the services of a competent professional should be sought. (From a Declaration of Principle jointly adopted by Committees of the American Bar Association and the American Publishers Association.)

This guide in no way constitutes a guarantee or promise to obtain a property tax reduction. It provides information and know-how instrumental to obtaining a reduction in the event of error, omission, or ignorance of circumstance on the part of the appraiser. The author believes the information herein to be correct, but he is not liable for error or omission.

# Save Thousands on Your Property Taxes!

# 1

# Tax Reduction Background and Process

## Unpopular Tax

On February 3, 1990, San Antonio, Texas, voters, by a margin of two to one, attempted to reduce their property taxes by 50 percent. Their vote reflected a survey revealing their perception that their Bexar County and San Antonio governments were bloated, inefficient, and capable of reducing the $800 million budget by 50 percent if the fat were cut out of local government. San Antonians are not unique. Proposals to limit the property tax have been put to popular vote in several states, and some have passed.

Over the past three years, 87 percent of local communities in the United States have raised real-estate taxes by an average of 24 percent. Property taxes in the 50 U.S. counties with the highest total revenues average $170 per year per person. But assessments vary widely, ranging from $27 in Hamilton County, Ohio, to $1,185 in Fairfax County, Virginia (D.C. area).

In many areas of Long Island, New York, real estate taxes have risen 85 percent since 1981, more than double the inflation rate during that period. A Gallup poll showed that in 1989, for the first time since 1978, the property tax was more distasteful to Americans than the income tax. Property tax is the "comeback kid of the 1980s," according to Steven Gold, director of fiscal studies for the National Conference of State Legislatures. In Texas a record 37 elections were held to force tax rollbacks in 1990. Taxes in the 37 areas were raised over 8 percent in one year. A statewide reassessment in Kansas sparked so much resentment that the governor has

1

proposed a constitutional amendment rolling back local property taxes 20 percent.

New Jersey voters rejected more school budgets in 1989 than in the previous 10 years. Taxes in the Maryland suburbs of Washington, D.C., have doubled in 10 years. "There's an increasing groundswell [of property tax resentment] in New Hampshire," says John Andrews, of the New Hampshire Muni (Town) Association. Joel Cogan of Connecticut's Muni Association echoes Andrews. Evidence of taxpayer mistrust and restlessness showed up when voters defeated proposed tax overhauls and educational and welfare increases in Louisiana, Pennsylvania, Oregon, Michigan, and Washington.

Several years ago, state governments were abandoning property tax as a revenue source, but recently increasing state revenue needs are reversing this trend.

Since state governments were relying less on property tax revenue, why does this unpopular, poorly administered property tax continue to be so important to local governments? The United States has a relatively productive, well-administered income tax. Retail sales taxes are also productive, with the proceeds usually going to the state. But property tax is crucial to local governments as a major source of revenue and as a "gap-closer" between budget needs and local government revenue. Property tax

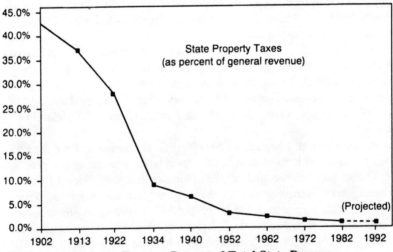

**Figure 1-1. Property Taxes as Percent of Total State Revenue**

(*Property Taxation Journal*, vol. 8, no. 2, p. 121).

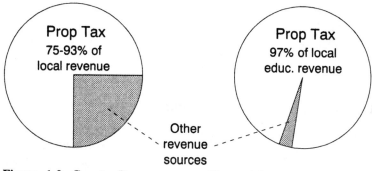

**Figure 1-2. County Property Taxes as a Percentage of Local Revenue**

(*Property Taxation Journal,* vol. 8, no. 2, p. 121).

**Figure 1-3. County Property Taxes as a Percentage of Local Education Revenue**

(*Property Taxation Journal,* vol. 8, no. 2, p. 121).

is usually levied in dollar amounts to balance the local government budget. (See Figures 1-1, 1-2, and 1-3.)

Figure 1-2 shows where more than 75 percent of the county dollars come from. Figure 1-3 shows where 97 percent of the local educational dollar comes from. The local educational dollar accounts for 42 cents of the entire education dollar; 50 cents comes from the state and 8 cents from Washington, D.C. (*Miami Herald,* 4/2/90, p. 12A).

## *Why You May Pay Too Much Property Tax*

Watch tonight's television newscast. You'll see jailbound thieves and lawyers, junkies, the homeless, AIDS victims, overwhelmed nurses, teachers, police, and judges, deteriorating roads and neighborhoods, polluted rivers and oceans . . . and a puff short, perhaps children at play or a heroic deed to leave you with an emotional high. The message comes through loud and clear: **Your government needs tax dollars now.**

Much of the money for police, firemen, roads, public hospitals, environmental cleanups, even immigrant needs, and 42 percent of school funding comes from your property taxes. Sales tax, occupational licenses, and phone bill surtaxes also help to a minor extent.

The assessor determines the value of all the real estate in the county. The county and city commissioners determine the millage. The tax on your home equals your assessor's estimated tax value, called *assessment,* times the applicable millage. For example, if your home's tax assessment is $100,000, and your tax district's millage is 40 mills, or 4 cents, your tax bill is $4,000 ($100,000 times 0.04).

## Appraised Versus Assessed Value

Be aware of a very important distinction: *Appraised* value is the **market value,** determined by a **bank or private value** appraisal. It is the estimate of the present sales price of your house. *Assessed* value is the **taxable value** determined by a **county or other government employee.** It is a percent of the estimated sales price of your house. Even though your county tax assessor may be called "county appraiser," and the two words are used interchangeably, they are different. For example, the **assessed value** may be 70 percent of the **market value;** thus a home **assessed** at $70,000 may **appraise** (or sell) for $100,000. (We discuss this later, under the topic "Coefficient of Dispersion.")

The county or city appraiser's bosses are the mayor, commissioners, managers, budget director, and other officials. They want the assessor to **increase** assessments, and thus revenue, because they are always short of funds. Often, a house with a market value between $90,000 and $100,000 tends to be assessed closer to $100,000 than to $90,000. The assessor knows that most people don't understand the property tax appeal process and don't take the time to find out about it. So the assessor tends to attach a high value to properties.

## The Assessor's Presumption of Correctness

The county or city assessor knows that **he** has the presumption of correctness. You may be thinking that this is just the opposite of American **criminal** law, under which the alleged wrongdoer is presumed innocent until proven guilty. You are right.

However, property tax law is **civil** law. This means that the tax assessment is presumed correct unless you can prove otherwise. It is up to you to prove that your property assessment is too high. The assessor has less reason to err on the low side and many reasons to favor the county treasury. If the assessor makes a mistake, it's usually in the city or county's favor. The alert taxpayer will remedy the error, but many people may not know that they are overpaying.

## Sources of Property Assessment Errors

The first line of the assessor's defense is: defend property tax assessments. Government can't afford to assess every house every year. It *mass assesses.* It looks at typical house sales in neighborhoods in every sector of the county. It also uses statistics on all county residential sales each quarter. Thus, it knows how much prices are going up or down in response to the business cycle. But many houses fall through the cracks and are overassessed.

The major reasons for granting lower assessments usually fall into three categories: **(1) physical deterioration, (2) external deterioration, and (3) functional obsolescence.** Examples of *(1) physical deterioration:* termites, roof leak, poor plumbing, lack of or inadequate air-conditioning, old electrical wiring, lack of or inadequate weather insulation; *(2) external deterioration* (also called economic, locational, environmental deterioration): planned nearby prison, junior or senior high school, expressway, heavily traveled street (air and noise pollution), economically depressed area, increasing crime, subject to flooding; *(3) functional obsolescence:* poor layout (for example, no bathroom window, kitchen access only through a bedroom), three bedrooms and only **one bath** (should be two), old kitchen or old bath.

Focus on the reasons for granting your home a tax assessment reduction to make your case. Proximity to high-voltage transmission wires, to a high school, or to a prison can build your case.

Suppose your home has 25-year-old wiring. It is not up to your city's 1990 building code. Surrounding homes may have been remodeled, and thus may be superior to yours. Get a copy of your electrical code and use it at your hearing.

## Appraisal Norms

Residential and commercial appraisal norms are now in fact regulated by government-sponsored agencies that are owned by the public. The Federal National Mortgage Association (FNMA), Federal Housing Administration (FHA), Federal Deposit Insurance Corporation (FDIC), and Resolution Trust Corporation (RTC) are only a few such entities.

The assessor doesn't have the facilities to discover that you spent $3,000 in repairs, or that your homesite happens to be the lowest in the area, subjecting it to flooding, or has other problems.

Assessors know that an FNMA appraisal norm holds that no house is worth more than 115 percent of the highest sale price in that neighborhood in the past year. Yet assessor computers are programmed to assess a house according to the house's square footage, even if the assessment is 150 percent of the value of the highest area sale price in the past year.

It is easy for an assessor to overlook important factors. For example, a 3,000-square-foot house in a 1,200-square-foot, $96,000, $80-per-square-foot neighborhood is often assessed at $80 per square foot times 3,000 square feet—$240,000. But $240,000 house-buyers purchase homes in $200,000 to $300,000 neighborhoods, not in $80,000 to $110,000 areas. So FNMA's highest loan in this neighborhood would be 115 percent of the highest sale price in the last year. If that highest sale was $135,000, the maximum market value for FNMA loan purposes would be 115 percent of $135,000, or $155,250.

Or an unimproved, 25-year-old house may be assessed at the same value per square foot as its completely remodeled 25-year-old neighbor. Computer glitches may also contribute to flawed assessments.

**Declining market** is another reason for an overassessment. When employers lay off large numbers of employees, home prices usually drop. Tax assessments often lag behind the market by several years. So if a 1990 layoff occurred in your area, your 1991 assessment very likely should be lower.

## Coefficient of Dispersion

In 1789, Congress decreed the first census of the United States, to occur in 1790. The purpose of the census was then and is now to apportion congressional representatives. But today there is other information available. For example, the 1990 census should have an accurate Coefficient of Dispersion, or CD. The CD is the ratio of the tax assessed value to the market/recent sales value. It is equal to the total assessment divided by the total sales of the assessed properties. Put another way, the CD compares the assessed value of properties with sale prices. Ideally, the sale price should be about 10 percent above the assessment value, when the assessment is supposed to be 90 percent of the value. Ten percent of the sale price goes for real estate and attorney fees and other costs, such as taxes. Find out if the 1990 census data has been incorporated into your assessor's database yet. If it has been incorporated, use it!

To be even more accurate, you can develop your own immediate neighborhood CD, **before you do your low-ball appraisal.** Take 30 recent house sales near you and calculate a CD on them. You can get the sale prices and assessments from a realtor or the local tax roll. Keep your source data in case you are asked for it. This will give you an overall picture. But remember, your house may still be overassessed because of such factors as a leaking roof, heavy traffic, a recent fire in the kitchen, needed repairs, or lack of applied-for exemptions. Call the 1-800 number of the Bureau of the Census, or your local federal information number, to zero in on the census data available in your area. (More on CDs in Chapter 2.)

## *The Board of Equalization*

The Board of Equalization (or BofE, aka Board of Assessment, Property Appraisal Adjustment Board or "PAAB," Board of Appeal, or the "Taxpayer's Friend") is the county agency in charge of executing and refereeing the procedures for tax appeals. It appoints the **special masters** (chief hearing officers), **sends out hearing notices, keeps records,** and **monitors hearings** to make sure that the taxpayer gets fair play. The **assessor's advocate** defends the assessment, thus opposing the **taxpayer.** The **special master** decides the case. The **BofE representative** is a silent observer at the hearing who can later file a complaint if the taxpayer is abused or if there is a violation of the state property appeals statute. **However, the BofE does not help the taxpayer prepare his case, or speak on his behalf at the hearing.**

To sum up, your state has assessment guidelines for the property-assessment-to-market-value ratio, which guide your county Board of Equalization (BofE). If an assessor is mandated with a 90 percent assessment-to-market-value ratio, a $100,000 sale price should have a $90,000 assessment; a 75 percent ratio mandate would mean this same house assessment should be $75,000.

## *The Assessor's Calendar*

State law almost always determines the schedule of events. Check **your** state law or county assessor's office to determine his schedule of events calendar. Your **jurisdiction** may vary chronologically but the sequence of events will be almost identical to the calendar below.

In many states, in mid–month eight the assessor mails out the **proposed property tax notices** (final bills are sent out several months later). This mailing usually triggers a 15- to 40-day period for public and private meetings for complaints and adjustments and for filing formal property tax appeals. One to six months later, the taxpayer receives an **appeals hearing notice** in the mail.

You are probably not familiar with the rest of the story. In Florida, for example, if you pay your tax bill by November 30 you get a 4 percent discount; if you pay by December 30, a 3 percent discount, and so on. An unpaid tax bill is delinquent on April 1. The first week in June, delinquent tax bills are auctioned on the courthouse steps as **tax liens or tax certificates** (see Chapter 8). In many states, the lien buyer is assured of an 11 percent to 16 percent return, beginning at the date of lien purchase.

## How to Obtain a Property Tax Reduction Before Filing an Appeal

Call your assessor's office first, then the Board of Equalization (BofE) to obtain an appeals form and instructions. You can use last year's form if the current year's form is unavailable. Check the appeals procedures. Read the instructions carefully; they often contain important information, such as whether the BofE has the power to **raise** as well as **lower** or leave unchanged your property tax assessment. (The BofE has no authority to raise or lower *taxes*; only property *assessments*.) Some states allow raising *and* lowering assessments, while other states allow only lowering assessments. If your BofE (or assessor) has the power to raise **as well as lower** assessments, a more circumspect course of action is suggested.

In many states, you prepare your case in January to March, six months before the August proposed tax notice mailing. Then you phone the assessor's office to schedule your 1991 tax assessment **pre-appeals conference.** A month or so after this informal meeting, you will probably receive a **notice of reduction.** This will show up on your **proposed tax notice.** Congratulations! You won without filing an appeal! (Examples of the notices and similar materials are given elsewhere in this book.)

After your assessor conference, the assessor may file a statement attesting to the fair market appraised value and the tax assessed value of the subject property. Then the BofE may either accept the assessor's values and change the present one, or reject the assessor's values and set or reset the appeal for a hearing. If this decision proves unsatisfactory to the taxpayer, a property tax reduction hearing procedure requires the BofE to: (1) have the taxpayer or agent make a presentation before the board; (2) examine under oath the taxpayer or agent appealing the assessment.

## *Review the Assessor's Data on Your Appeal*

Several weeks before your appeal date, or a month or so after you file your appeal, call the assessor's office to find out if you can review the material the assessor has on your case. In most cases you can examine it. If you can photocopy it do so, otherwise take notes on what issues the assessor is defending. Then gather what information you can to build your case. If the assessor says you cannot see what he has prepared, check with your county clerk. The Freedom of Information Act should enable you to obtain this public information and you have a good reason to look at it. The only thing the assessor may withhold is personal notes he jotted down concerning your case, and in many instances, you can examine these too.

## *The Appeals Hearing*

The appeals hearing is an adversarial process. If you are not satisfied with the results of your prehearing conference, file an appeal during the designated period. You will get a hearing notice several weeks or months later. This hearing, a quasijudicial procedure, is chaired by a *special master*. First, you are sworn in and present your case, with data supporting a reduction. (You already submitted this material to the BofE or the assessor's office, either with your appeal or at least five working days before the hearing.) Then the *county assessor's advocate* makes his case, with data supporting "no change" (no reduction) in your property assessment. A *BofE representative* monitors the procedure, and often a *court reporter* records it. You must prove that the county appraiser made a mistake, omitted relevant data, did not consider a circumstance that lowers the value of your home (use receipts or estimates of house repairs), used a misprogrammed computer, or incorrectly denied your exemption. This process is like a tug-of-war. Both sides pull as hard as they can. But if you do your homework, you will probably win.

In more informal counties, a recorder may replace the court reporter and there may be no BofE representative. There, you are with the special master and the assessor's advocate only. In the simplest procedure, which often occurs in sparsely populated counties, it's just you and the county property assessor.

Should the special master rule **"no change"** (no reduction), you have the right to file suit in the state board of appeal (if your state has one), a higher quasijurisdiction than your local BofE. Next, you can file a complaint in your state court system (small claims, circuit, or superior court), either with or without prejudice to the hearing results (check your state regulations). Your next appeal levels are your district court of appeal and finally your state supreme court.

## *Making the Most of Your Property Tax Reduction Opportunity*

The naive taxpayer tells the special master: "My taxes are too high; I can't afford it because . . ." he is retired, unemployed, sick, and so forth. Unfortunately, this approach does not reduce tax assessments. A special master who consistently grants more than a token reduction will not be reappointed the following year. However, retirement, illness, or unemployment *may* be cause for a tax *exemption,* depending on your state statutes and county or city ordinances.

A successful appeal for a tax reduction is the result of the taxpayer overcoming the assessor's valuation, which is presumed correct, by showing evidence that similar houses in his own and nearby similar neighborhoods are selling for less than his home's assessment. He also can show that his house needs repairs, such as a new roof, termite extermination, or a new air-conditioner. **Proving your case, however, is easier than you realize. Four out of five petitioners obtain hefty tax reductions.**

# 2

---

# Tax Reduction Petition Concepts

These concepts help you master the procedure for reducing your taxes.

## Folio Numbers

You should familiarize yourself with folio numbers, also called property identification numbers (PINs) or property IDs (PIDs), as time permits. The folio number is your house's tax identification number, like your Social Security number. It is a geographical classification too complex to analyze here in detail.

After the American Revolution, our Confederation of States needed to rapidly sell the land it acquired through purchases and treaties. On May 25, 1785, the government passed a land ordinance establishing the rectangular or government survey system of 6-by-6-mile, or 36-square-mile, townships. This system became the principal legal survey system for most land west of the Ohio and Mississippi rivers and for Florida, Mississippi, and Alabama. But the curvature of the earth, original survey error, and other discrepancies create "extra land." These areas are called "Government Lots." If your property is in a Government Lot, the section number will be 37 or higher. This is explained below.

The meaning of a property's folio number, for example, **30 5105 061 0087,** is briefly this: **30,** municipality or county area; **5,** last digit of two-digit (55) township; **1,** last digit of two-digit (41) range; **05,** section; **061,** subdivision number; **0087,** parcel number. Six-mile-long townships

11

run north-south; six-mile-wide ranges east-west. There are 36 one-mile sections (6 miles by 6 miles) in a township-range. If a Government Lot is between two townships, it will carry the township and range number above (not below) it; the section will be section 37 or higher. Each section is one square mile. Sometimes the township-range (ours is 51, above) of 36 square miles is referred to as "township 51," even though it really is township 55, **range 41.** Find 5106, township 55, range 41, section 5 in Figure 2-1. It is marked. (Look at the subdivision plat in the raw data of Case 1 for further clarification.)

Figure 2-2 shows a parcel roughly 12 miles by 12 miles. Each square is a township, 6 by 6 miles, or 36 miles square. One of the townships is divided into its 36 sections, each one square mile. Find Section 11 in Township 1 North Range 1 East. It is just south of Section 2 (5,280 linear feet equal 1 linear mile, as the full section indicates). Find "A" in this section. A is in the lower square, labeled Full Section, on the right side just above the middle. To locate it according to the metes and bounds method, start with the last item and move toward the first one—that is, start with the NE 1/4 or NE/4, and work your way to the SW/4.

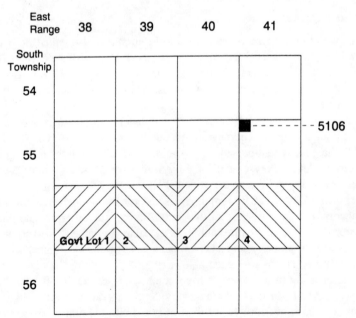

**Figure 2-1. Townships, Ranges, Sections, and Government Lots.**

# U.S. Public Survey Diagram

## Four Townships

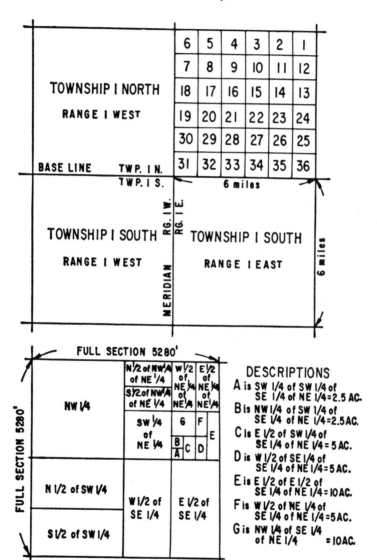

Figure 2-2. U.S. Public Survey Diagram.

Plats are survey maps. Your city map scale usually contains a line indicating that "one inch = 2 (or 3, 4, etc.) miles." This neighborhood plat has a scale indicating that one inch = 200 feet. It is in the upper right quadrant. The scale is no longer correct because the plat was reduced for publication.

The circled numbers are blocks; small lot numbers appear sporadically; 1, 2, 7, 13, 25. One and two are often marked to indicate clockwise or counterclockwise numbering. Occasionally an address appears; 17434 NW 63 Ct.

An ideally shaped lot width is 50 to 60 percent of its length. The frontage is just over half of its depth. Examples of ideally shaped lots are just right of the second "n" in Mediterranean Blvd. However, block 12 lots, on the other side of Med. Blvd., are "wet," or waterfront, lots. The waterfront asset outweighs the best-shaped-lot asset. This makes the wet lots the most valuable in the subdivision.

In Figure 2-3, can you find 17424 NW 63rd Ct.? It is Block 7, Lot 24. You almost need a magnifying glass, but the lot dimensions (42 by 113) are distinguishable. Dittos mean the nearby lots are the same dimensions. Find Block 12, Lot 3. It is 17332 NW 63rd Ct. Does Block 6, Lot 21 face Mediterranean Blvd.? (No.) Why? (To escape heavy traffic.) The county record plat (map) of this subdivision can be found in Plat Book 127, on page 15 (this is indicated in parentheses on 174 Way).

Your assessor's office will be glad to introduce you to the vagaries of your area. Once you see the maps and layout, you will not find it as mysterious as it may appear here. But at least you are now familiar with plats.

## Comparable Sales Selection

The property map, or plat, in Figure 2-3 contains lot sizes and dimensions. You can compare your lot size to the size of the comparable sales lot sizes, and thus compare land assessments. What kind of sales do you need? Comparable sales must be sufficiently near in time and location, and sufficiently similar in respect to size, character, situation, usability, and zoning or other legal restriction so that it is clear that the properties are cash equivalent, or substitutable (principle of substitution).

## Coefficient of Dispersion

In Chapter 1 we learned that the CD is the assessed value divided by the market value—that is, assessments (numerator) divided by sales prices

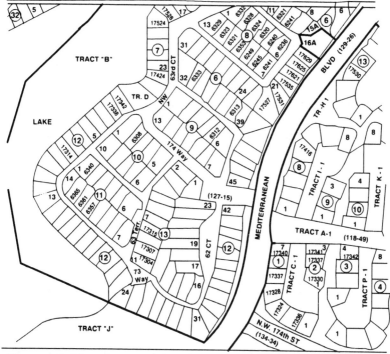

**Figure 2-3. Plat with Block Numbers Circled, Lots with Numbers and Addresses.**

(denominator). For example, if the 1990 total assessment value of 30 houses in your neighborhood was $2.7 million, and the total sales prices of these units was $3 million, the assessment value of the houses was 90 percent of the sales prices. The CD was 0.9 or 90 percent in that zip code (or other designated area). You may be thinking that the 1990 census will be outdated by 1991. For our purposes you are right. But your assessor keeps tabs on his area CDs monthly, even weekly. Sometimes politics distorts the CD, so you are best off running a check of a dozen or so recent area sales yourself.

Now apply this information to your situation. Remember, your house's appraised value is $100,000, and its assessed value is $90,000. You check your local property tax assessor office and find that:

1. The mandated CD should be 0.9. Your appraiser deserves an accolade.

2. The mandated CD should be 0.7. The 0.9 or 90 percent CD assessments are 20 percent too high (in your case, $20,000 too high). Cause for action, maybe even class action.

3. The mandated CD should be 100 percent. The assessment of $90,000 is too low; let sleeping dogs lie.

An increased CD may be mandated directly by state statute, or indirectly by a federal judge to build a new county prison, to desegregate a school system, or to put in a new local water system.

Your assessment will probably vary from the mandated assessment. One reason for reading this book is to see if your house is above the norm, or CD. If it is, you have a good opportunity to save money. To do this, you will need, among other things, to compare houses' square footage.

## Adjusted Square Feet

Assessors value houses in dollars per square foot. Often your folio or Property Identification Number card/printout in the assessor's office will list your **"adjusted square feet"** (asf). This is distinct from your **living square feet (lsf)**. Your **asf includes your lsf.** Look at the most common formula for asf in Figure 2-4, a *strange* house, but one that gets the point across. It comprises 100 percent of the heated and air-conditioned area, 50 percent of the garage and storeroom, and 33 percent of the porch. The **1,183 asf,** as you can see, **includes** the **900 lsf.** Since the assessor prefers asf, you must use asf.

Your assessor's office almost always has a dollar value per square foot for homes in a subdivision. If the aforementioned strange house is in New York, and the assigned value of the house is $50 per square foot, and the

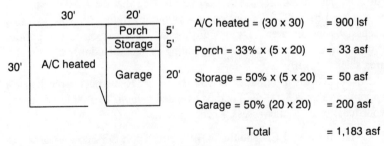

**Figure 2-4. Adjusted Square Feet Determination.**

lot is $100 per square foot, its assessed value is 1,183sf times $50 per sf, or $59,150. A pool, if there were one, would probably add $8,000.

The land value is assessed the same way. Suppose your lot is 60 feet by 100 feet—6,000 sf. If the dollar value is $200 per square foot, the lot value is $1.2 million. You probably own a brownstone in a good New York neighborhood. Ordinarily, your lot value should be 20 percent to 35 percent of your building's assessment. However, if you live in Malibu or Pacific Palisades this example is probably understated.

In sum, use your assessor's asf to find your comparables. Use the formulas above to check your own house's asf against the one on your tax bill.

## Millage

A mill is a tenth of a cent. Therefore, 10 mills make one cent. Sometimes the millage is not explicitly stated. Look at your tax bill and find your new (1) total proposed tax and (2) total tax assessment. To determine millage, divide 1 by 2. When you are preparing for your prehearing conference with the assessor, use the latest numbers available. They will be close enough. Many counties have printed millage tables now. Ask for one from the assessor's office.

## How Your Property Tax Is Determined

In the illustration below, we use month names and county government for simplicity. If your tax assessment year begins in May, you must add five months to the example. January in the example is May in your county (or city).

Check your county's governing body, such as the board of commissioners. It determines a tentative, proposed tax millage about five months (May) into the tax assessment process. (The month will vary in the different towns and cities in your county.) The board does this by weighing the proposed county expenses against the anticipated county revenue. In August, the assessor mails out the proposed tax bill. The millage of your county will often be "written in stone" in September or October. Your proposed tax bill, which you receive in month eight, is just that: proposed. Your final bill arrives in November. If you meet with your assessor in the months of January to May, use the previous year's millage table. This will not affect your arguments for a tax reduction. If you obtain a reduction in the spring of 1993 using the 1993 millage rate, your August proposed tax bill will incorporate your assessment reduction, but it will have the proposed new 1993 millage rate.

Suppose you are *not* Mike Tyson, Ivana Trump, Johnny Carson, or even one of the former Mrs. Carsons. You don't live in Malibu and your proposed property tax bill shows that the total proposed tax rate is 26 mills, or 2.6 cents, for every assessed dollar. Your total assessment for improvements plus your land is $100,000. Therefore, .026 times $100,000 equals $2,600 taxes owed.

Enrico Sanchez's house is three miles from you. His assessment is also $100,000, and his millage is 22.0430. Mr. Sanchez's tax notice indicates taxes of .022043 times $100,000, or $2,204.30.

## Guarding Against Large Tax Increases

A 1990 Supreme Court ruling (*Missouri* v. *Jenkins*) grants federal judges the authority to order local tax increases for education, prisons, health, housing, welfare, ecology, and other reasons. At this writing it appears that this ruling could eventually be restricted to civil rights, but it augurs higher property taxes.

Many county assessor public relations departments issue pre-property-tax-mailing press releases that read "Tax rates to remain the same this year" (translation: Assessments will rise), or "Assessments to remain the same this year" (translation: Millage tax rates will rise).

You could receive a 1 percent to 30 percent increase this year, or no increase. Tax increases vary widely with local community and location. Find out what your area residential tax rate increase is. Then get out last year's final mortgage statement or tax bill and compare assessments and millages. Is the assessment proportionately higher? If your assessment is the same, check your millage. Is the proposed millage proportionately higher? Your local newspaper always has tax reports on property tax explaining where the increases will come from, so keep an eye out for this information.

If you have a 10 percent or more tax jump there may well be a mistake. You may have a case for reduction. By monitoring your tax bills annually you alert yourself to possible assessor errors.

## Apples Versus Oranges, or, Tax Assessment Reductions Versus Property Tax Exemptions

Exemptions are unrelated to assessment reductions. You may not have applied for an exemption due you. Or your exemption may not have been recorded, or may have been understated. Many counties have homestead, veterans, widow, senior citizen, and disabled exemptions.

Does your tax bill contain the exemptions you are entitled to? A homestead (primary residence) exemptee whose property is assessed at $80,000 may have a $10,000, $25,000, or even higher exemption. Check your assessor's office to find out about the types of exemptions your county has. The author recently alerted a totally disabled veteran to 100 percent property exemption, which applies in many states. Although the veteran will pay no more property taxes, he cannot recover the taxes he paid in previous years.

Reductions and exemptions can lead to substantial savings for you. But you have to build a case by using data acceptable to the "system." Some examples follow, starting with the role of mortgages and property insurance in building your case.

## Mortgages and Property Insurance Policies

You acquire an edge when you understand **basic mortgage finance.** For example, a $100,000 mortgage at 11 percent with a 30-year term has a principal and interest payment of $952.32 per month. At the end of year one, you have paid $10,978 interest and $450 principal. At the end of year five, when the average person sells his home, you have paid $54,304 interest and $2,835 principal. You therefore still owe a principal of

**Table 2-1. Tax Reduction and Exemption.**

|  | House A (No Exemption) | House B ($25,000 Homestead Exemption) |
| --- | --- | --- |
| Tax Assessment | $100,000 | $100,000 |
| Tax Assessment Reduction | (20,000) | (20,000) |
| Homestead Exemption | 0 | (25,000) |
| Taxable Amount of Assessment | 80,000 | 55,000 |
| Tax Bill at 26 Mills | 2,080 | 1,430 |
| Savings from Exemption Alone | 0 | 650 |

$97,165, because you pay mostly **interest** when the mortgage is new, and mostly principal as the loan matures. You can pay off a 30-year mortgage in 12 to 15 years by making roughly the same mortgage payment (say, $1,000 per month) every two weeks ($500 every other week). Your payments would be about 16 percent higher than they are now. Check this out with a mortgage broker when you have time and want to increase your investment in your home.

Look at your **mortgage(s)** and **property insurance policies.** If you just purchased your house, you probably don't have an insurance policy. You may have your lender's private mortgage insurance (PMI), which is often an integral part of your mortgage. It insures the lender, should the purchaser die. However, if your mortgage is over five years old, you may have purchased a real property insurance policy to protect the increased value of your house since you obtained your first mortgage. Fixtures, or appurtenances, are bolted, screwed, planted in the ground, or glued to the building and are a taxable part of real estate. Personal property, such as furniture, jewelry, electronic devices, and other **"nonfixture"** articles not screwed, bolted, or connected by pipes to the building are not a subject of home assessment.

Photocopy the title and "amount insured" pages of the mortgage(s) and property insurance policy. Your appraiser or an item on the BofE petition form will usually request them. This is why. If you have an 80 percent loan-to-value $90,000 mortgage with a $22,500 down payment on your four-year-old house and are protesting a $101,000 assessment, the county assessor will add $22,500 ($90,000 divided by 0.8, minus $90,000) to the original mortgage, to obtain the original sale price of the house, $112,500. He then deducts 10 percent selling costs ($11,250) to obtain the $101,250 assessed value (see Table 2-2). Note that we assume the assessor's coefficient of dispersion or CD mandate is 90 percent of market value.

Since the calculated assessed value is close to the actual assessed value, all is not lost, but you have some work to do. For example, if you can show

**Table 2-2. How Your Mortgage Principal Indicates Sale Price.**

| | |
|---|---|
| 80% mortgage | $ 90,000 |
| Down payment | 22,500 [($90,000/.8) − $90,0000] |
| Sale price | 112,500 |
| 10% Selling cost | (11,250) |
| Assessment | **101,250 (or $112,000 if CD is 100%)** |

that property values have declined in your neighborhood, you have a case for a tax assessment reduction.

Now consider an overassessed house. If you recently applied for a maximum loan and obtained an 80 percent loan-to-value first mortgage for $60,000 and your house is assessed at $100,000, you have a case for a $32,500 reduction. Why? Your lender's appraisal, with recent sales, probably came in at or a little above $75,000. Eighty percent of $75,000 is $60,000, which is your mortgage principal. If you deduct 10 percent selling costs, $7,500, from $75,000 you get the proper county assessed value of $67,500. The assessed value of $100,000 less $67,500 equals a $32,500 reduction in assessment (see Table 2-3).

Property insurance ordinarily covers up to 80 percent of the market value of a new house. If you have a 10-year-old, 80 percent loan-to-value (LTV) ratio $50,000 mortgage, and a 6-month-old $100,000 (building only) property insurance policy, your house's value is $100,000 divided by 0.8, or $125,000. Deducting 10 percent ($12,500) for selling costs yields a tax assessed value of $112,000 (rounded down). Your 10-year-old mortgage is irrelevant to the house's present value, but the LTV ratio is not. Your LTV ratio has probably decreased quite a bit over the years due to inflation, if nothing else, unless you live in the oil patch.

The amount of your mortgage can be crucial to your appeal, especially if it is less than two years old. Sometimes there is a second or even a third mortgage on the property. Mortgages are public documents, recorded at the courthouse, and as such are accessible for title searches. This means that the assessor's advocate may have a copy. Almost all densely populated counties have computerized property data. Lying or submitting falsified documents under oath in this quasijudicial proceeding is perjury, a criminal offense. It is not a recommended course of action. If the special master or your petition form requests your IRS 1040 Schedule A, listing your mortgage interest deductions, you may have a slight problem should you have neglected to mention a nonrecorded private mortgage. More on this later.

**Table 2-3. Assessment Determination via Recent Mortgage.**

| | |
|---|---|
| 80% mortgage | $60,000 |
| Down payment | 15,000 [$60,000/.8) − $60,000] |
| Sale price | 75,000 |
| Less 10% selling cost | 7,500 |
| Assessment | **67,500** (or **$75,000** if CD is 100%) |

**Table 2-4. Second Mortgage Lender's Collateral.**

| | |
|---|---|
| Year 6 first mortgage | $  30,000 |
| Year 6 first mortgage (principal) | 48,500    ($50,000 − $1,500) |
| Second lender's thinking | $78,500/0.7 = $112,143 (current market value) |

Suppose you have an 80 percent (normal for 1984), $50,000, 9 percent interest, six-year-old first mortgage and a $30,000 new second mortgage on your house. Your dwelling is worth at least $100,000. You should familiarize yourself with mortgage loan amortization schedules. For example, a 1985 80 percent first mortgage of $50,000 (mortgage principal) shows $50,000 divided by 0.8, or $62,000 original market value. The original market value is based on the sale price and the lender's appraisal at that time. This was the **bank-appraised valuation.** You have paid about $1,571 of the **principal.** The rest of your payment went to interest.

The second lender appraised your house at $112,000 to $115,000 before making his $30,000 loan. He rarely lends above 70 percent loan to value. He feels that, should he have to enter foreclosure proceedings against you, not only will his principal and interest be protected, but also his legal fees. The 10 percent selling cost will also be covered by the sale of the property. In all likelihood, your second mortgage has a clause to this effect. Your primary (first-mortgage) lender has a **nonsubordination** clause, which means that he gets his principal plus interest **first.** This relieves him of the anxiety of having some other lender "bump" (precede) him. However, should the Internal Revenue Service put a lien on the property, its lien often precedes all others, including that of the primary lender. Other governmental liens are inferior to, or subordinated to, IRS, but superior to private lenders.

To sum up with our example above:

| | |
|---|---|
| $112,143 | Current market value |
| Times 0.9 | Selling allowance fees |
| Equals $100,929 | After fees |
| Minus $48,500 | First lender loan |
| Equals $52,429 | Remaining equity after 1st mortgage |
| Minus $30,000 | Second lender loan |
| Equals $22,429 | Owner equity after second mortgage |

The $22,429 owner equity represents the risk the owner takes. If the market should drop 15 percent, the lenders are still protected.

## Warranty Deed and IRS Form 1040, Schedule A, Lines 9a and 9b

Your *warranty deed* is the legal document that guarantees that you own your house. It often contains the amount, date of purchase, and other information. Copies of the cover page and germane information (amount and date of purchase) for deeds less than two years old can be critical to your case. Sometimes the warranty deed has the sales tax stamps on it. If the tax is 2 percent of the purchase price, and you can see a $1,000 stamp, you know the sale price was $50,000.

If your warranty deed or other document shows you purchased a house in 1991 for $75,000, and its 1992 assessment is $100,000, you are almost assured of a $25,000 property assessment reduction, because your 1992 assessment is based upon 1991 sales in most states. Your house is assessed as of January 1 of the tax year.

Now, return to the unrecorded second or third mortgages, as they may present a problem. Your **IRS Form 1040, Schedule A, lines 9a and 9b,** is required on some appeals forms. For example, Mr. G has a 10-year-old $50,000 bank mortgage at 10 percent interest, with a 29-year term, duly recorded at the courthouse. Three years ago he obtained a private, $30,000 second mortgage that is unrecorded. Mr. G is attempting to reduce his tax assessment of $80,000 to $70,000. The assessor can pull up the first $50,000 mortgage on the computer (or look it up), but not the $30,000 private second mortgage because it's not recorded. However, his home

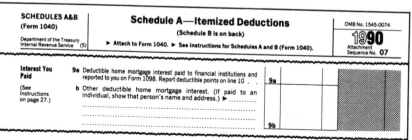

**Figure 2-5. IRS Form 1040, Schedule A, Showing Mortgage Interest Deductions.**

interest deductions on the first mortgage show up on IRS Form 1040, Schedule A, line 9A, and on the second mortgage on line 9B.

Many BofE petition forms request 1040 Schedule A; a few do not. Omitting a Schedule A can weaken your case. If Mr. G fails to mention or include the second mortgage, he risks perjury and fraud charges.

## Next Year—Taxes up Again

The property assessor is under continuing pressure to raise property assessments to maintain and expand city and county services. When you successfully reduce your 1991 assessment, you may find that your 1992 tax is the original 1991 tax plus a 15 percent tax increase, or 115 percent of your original, prereduction 1991 assessment. So you should repeat the whole procedure next year.

## Property Tax Appeal Event Sequence

Most counties have deadlines for appealing assessments and will not grant **chronological exceptions. It's easy to miss a deadline. Table 2-5 is a typical calendar.** Your jurisdiction's (county's) property taxpayer event calendar may vary from this one, but the event sequence will be identical, or nearly so.

Summary of discounts if property tax bill received November 20:

| | |
|---|---|
| If paid before December 1 | 4% discount |
| If paid before January 1 | 3% |
| If paid before February 1 | 2% |
| If paid before March 1 | 1% |
| If paid before April 1 | 0% |

In some jurisdictions, all the BofE appeals are complete by end of month 12 (EoM12). In other places, appeals extend until month 20, the eighth month of the following year.

Successful tax petitioners are automatically granted the full payment discount. Unsuccessful petitioners are subject to the same discount calendar that governs nonpetitioners. (For example, if you had a January 1993 hearing with a resultant no change determination that you received in the mail in February, and had not yet paid your bill, you would only be eligible for the February 1993, 1 percent discount.) Therefore it pays to remit the sum of the initial discounted bill early, and wait for the city or county refund of the difference.

**Table 2-5. Sequence of Property Tax Appeal Events.**

| Example Only | Dates Used in This Text | Events |
|---|---|---|
| Jan.–May 1991 | Months 1–5 | You prepare your case. |
| | Months 3–8 | You get a prehearing conference and hope for a satisfactory reduction. The county commission determines a tentative, proposed millage for your jurisdiction. |
| Aug. 17–19 | Month 8 | You receive your proposed tax notice. It's appeal-filing time. If your prehearing conference was successful, your reduced assessment will appear on this notice. |
| Sept. 18 | Month 9 | Deadline for filing appeals. |
| Oct. 31 | Month 10 | County commission sets final millage for your jurisdiction. |
| Nov. 10 | Month 11 | Final tax bill arrives. You pay your bill by end of Month 11 to obtain the 4 percent discount. In some states, you pay 50 percent plus of your bill if you appeal, and the remainder after the results of your appeal are evident. |
| Nov.–Dec. and Jan.–Aug. 1992 | Months 10–20 | Appeals hearings are conducted, and revised bills are mailed out. |
| May–June 1992 | Months 17–18 | If your appeal is successful, you get a discount automatically, so you get a refund of the lowered, discounted assessment. If unsuccessful, you still obtain your full 4 percent discount. |

You might handle your payment this way. You file your appeal August 21 (month 8), two days after receiving your proposed tax notice, and only three days into the appeal filing period. You receive your appeal hearing notice, set for November 15 (month 11). The special master grants you an assessment reduction (remember, he has no authority over millage). You know your final, reduced-assessment bill will arrive in February (month 14), with the automatically discounted 4 percent because the reduction was granted. But your income tax situation dictates that you pay by December 31. What do you do?

Multiply your area's millage by the total **reduced** assessment times 96 percent (your 4 percent discount) to get your new tax bill. Mail it to the address on the tax bill, **along with a copy of the special master's finding** (tax assessment reduction notice).

Usually everybody is happy. The city or county gets its money earlier than expected, and you maximize your income tax reduction for the year. The worst that can happen is that the county (or city) may send your check back and ask you to wait until they process your reduced bill. In this case, you may pay the unreduced bill and wait for your refund (often several months). Check your county treasurer or assessor first to determine the exact procedure and rules that apply to you.

# 3

# How to Determine
# if Your Home
# Is Overassessed

The two most successful approaches to reducing your tax assessment are the comparable sales analysis approach and, if permitted, the needed or completed repairs approach. If the completed repairs approach is permitted in your case, the two methods will reinforce each other. The comparable sales analysis approach is the most important because it normally leads to the greatest reduction.

The *comparable sales analysis* approach, illustrated here using Mr. Alpha's house, includes filing an appeal and attending the hearing. You can use this procedure to determine what your house assessment should be. A 26-mill tax rate is used in this example.

Table 3-1 is extremely important for understanding the process of estimating the correct assessed value. Examine it carefully. (In Table 3-1, "< ¼" means less than one-quarter acre. An acre is 43,560 square feet, so this means the lot is less than 10,890 square feet. Use the actual square footage if lot sizes vary more than 20 percent to 25 percent. The mean is the average. For example, the mean of 5, 10 and 20 is 35 divided by 3, or 11.67.)

From the data in Table 3-1, we can make the following computation:

**Comp average \$/sf = [\$75.00 + \$76.52 + \$70.37] ÷ 3 = \$73.96; \$73.96 × Subj 1,200 sf × 0.9 = \$79,952, rounded to \$80,000 = subject value; proposed true potential assessment reduction = \$100,000 − \$80,000 = \$20,000 (the assessment reduction) × \$.026 (26 mills) = \$520 potential tax dollar saving from comparable sales analysis.**

**Table 3-1. Master Example of a Comparable Sales Analysis.**

| Row | Item | Subject | Comparable 1 | Comparable 2 | Comparable 3 |
|---|---|---|---|---|---|
| 1 | Address[1] | 523 Elm St. | 520 Elm St. | 340 Oak St. | 980 3rd St. |
| 2 | Sales Price[2] | $100,000[3] | $90,000 | $88,000 | $95,000 |
| 3 | Square Feet[4] | 1,200 | 1,200 | 1,150 | 1,350 |
| 4 | Price per Square Foot[5] | $83.33 | $75.00 | $76.52 | $70.37 |
| 5 | Lot size (acres)[6] | < 1/4 | < 1/4 | < 1/4 | < 1/4 |
| 6 | Sale Date[7] | NA | 5/89 | 9/89 | 1/89 |
| 7 | Beds/baths[8] | 3/2 | 3/2 | 3/2 | 3/2 |
| 8 | DistFrSub[1] | 0 | 50 yds N | 2 blks NW | 6 blks SE |
| 9 | Year Built | 1980 | 1981 | 1955 | 1983 |
| 10 | Other | | Same Model As Sub | Remodeled[9] | Similar area |

[1] Comparables should be within 1.5 miles of subject.

[2] Sales price and living and adjusted square feet (referred to as sf) should be within 15 percent of subject, to conform to assessor guidelines.

[3] This $100,000 is the tax assessed value of the subject, not the sale price. The subject has not sold. We have premised a 100 percent CD for this example.

[4] You can use "apples," living sf, or "oranges," adjusted sf (takes in garage, and so forth), but don't mix apples and oranges in your presentation.

[5] Row 2 ÷ Row 3 = Row 4; comparable 1 $90,000 ÷ 1,200 sf = $75/sf.

[6] Lot size: Check lot prices when lots are more or less than 20 percent of subject lot. Usually the above is sufficient.

[7] The comparable sales have occurred in the 12 months before January 1, 1991. In a pinch, you can use sales from the 1991 first or second quarter.

[8] For a 3/1 (3 bed, 1 bath), add $2,000 to bring it up to subject's 3/2. Always adjust comparable up or down to subject. **Never** adjust subject up or down. This type of adjustment is optional.

[9] Older comparable 2 remodeling job makes it comparable to newer houses.

(If mandated, you can deduct 10 percent of the sale price for sale costs. Thus the 0.9, or 90 percent, in this example.)

Note 8 in Table 3-1 refers to the difference between a 3/1 bath and a 3/2 bath. The $2,000 is the assigned value differential between houses that are identical except for the extra bath in one. Another example not in Table 3-1: A house with a finished 30 by 30 basement (900 square feet) in your area may sell for $12,000 more than an identical house with an unfinished basement. Remember to always **adjust the comparables to the subject; never vice versa.**

*Needed repairs* is the second approach to determining if your home is overassessed. In 1990 Mr. Alpha has his leaking, 30-year-old roof replaced for $6,000. He also rewired his house for $1,500. The plumber told him his kitchen plumbing was bad, and gave him a $750 estimate to fix it. All Mr. Alpha's contractors are **licensed, bonded, and insured,** often a requirement for reduction. Alpha's 1991 tax year repairs are the following 1990 items:

| | |
|---|---:|
| Roof repairs | $6,000 |
| Rewiring | $1,500 |
| Plumbing | $ 750 |
| Total repairs | $8,250 |

The tax assessed value is $100,000 minus $8,250 repairs, or $91,750 potential proper assessed value.

Adding Mr. Alpha's sales comparison analysis and repair values produces a $28,000 potential reduction:

| | |
|---|---|
| Tax assessed value | $100,000 |
| Less sales analysis assessment reduction | $20,000 |
| Less repairs assessment reduction | $8,250 |
| Total potential assessment reduction | **$28,000** (rounded reduction) |
| 26 mills times $28,000 | $728 potential tax saving |

If the special master reduces the assessment, the tax savings is **$728.** Again, note that your **1991 repairs** apply to your **August 1992 proposed tax bill. 1991 sales values** apply to the **1992 tax year.** However, you may use first or second quarter 1991 comparable sales values if you don't have access to 1991 sales data. In a few states you may use 1992 repairs and sales for 1992 tax appeals. Check **your** state ruling on this.

Now change the example. Assume the three comparable sales average

$110,000 instead of $80,000. In this case, your $100,000 tax assessment is correct. Why? Because the assessed value in this example is the sales price less 10 percent for marketing costs. The $110,000 average value less **10 percent sales expense of $11,000 equals $99,000,** close enough!

## Allocation or Abstraction

Sometimes you must determine the value of your lot indirectly because there are no recent lot sales in your area. One way to determine such a value is by allocation. You can go to your supermarket to find out how allocation works. Your receipt says "Produce $1.00" for your apple and banana. If you see a sign saying APPLES $0.75 EACH, you know your banana costs a quarter. This is called "allocation," or "abstraction" in appraising. The total assessment on your property is the $1.00 for produce. The lot value that you obtained by allocation is $1.00 minus $0.75, or $0.25. Your improvement (building) is the apple cost of 75 cents.

## Appeal of Land Value Only, Using Allocation

First, ask your assessor whether you are allowed to appeal your land value exclusive of your building (and vice versa). If you find that you can appeal one and exclude the other, make sure you obtain a note from an official, preferably on official stationery, stating so. Or this option may be indicated in the instructions for filing an appeal.

For example, suppose you want to determine whether your land **or** improvements are excessively assessed. Your tax assessment notice or tax bill looks like this:

| | |
|---|---|
| Land | $35,000 |
| Improvements | $45,000 |
| Total Value | $80,000 |

Your premised CD is 80 percent (0.8), so your home's market value should be $100,000.

Here is the allocation procedure for estimating the value of your lot without the improvements:

1. Find recent sales of similar vacant lots in your (or a similar) neighborhood.
2. Find recent sales of homes similar to yours in your (or a similar) neighborhood.

3. Divide lot sale average by home sale average to obtain a ratio indicating allocated lot value.

For example: lot average value of $25,000 divided by home average value of $100,000 yields a ratio of 1/4. This ratio allocation of ¼ times your total assessed value is $25,000. But your tax notice indicates a lot value of $35,000. Your appeal is based upon a $10,000 lot overassessment. Your house is assessed at less than market value, but this is not the issue. If the assessor says, "That doesn't mean anything, the total value is what counts," your rebuttal is that he has erred and you are entitled to your land assessment reduction. Your state's BofE/appraisal statute usually indicates that both must be equitably assessed, or else they would not be itemized. Only the total assessment would appear.

Of course, if available, you could simply use the lot sales as evidence. But in some situations, allocation will be your only option.

## How to Obtain Data on Your Property; Property Record Card

When you call your assessor, ask for a copy of your *property record card*. This card contains information that will help you compare your house and lot with others. It will probably have a sketch of your house, with such pertinent information as adjusted square feet, bedrooms and baths, year built, and whether there is a pool.

## Excess Living or Lot Square Feet

After obtaining a copy of your property record card you measure your house and lot. Your house's square footage is measured from the outside (condos are measured from the inside). If the assessor's numbers are excessive, you are due an assessment reduction. This is because the assessor determines a particular property assessment by multiplying its lot square footage by what he determines is the average value per square foot in the area, and follows the same process for its living square footage. For example, if your measurements show that you have a 70 by 100 foot lot with a 1,600 living square footage house on it, and the assessor's data show a 100 by 100 lot worth $50,000, you are due a $15,000 reduction (7,000 divided by 10,000) times $50,000, or $35,000.

Your lot may be irregular, containing "excessive footage" or an area not easily usable. An ideal lot is square or broadly rectangular, because this maximizes the use of the lot. A 70 by 100 foot lot is ideal for the average 1,500 to 2,000 square foot house. Areas like the shaded areas shown in Figure 3-1 may provide a basis for obtaining a reduction in assessed value.

## How to Obtain Comparables

Ask your realtor for comparable sales information. Also, look in your community newspapers, and in the Homes For Sale magazines on racks outside realty offices and supermarkets. Look for realtor ads offering to estimate the value of your house, because the realtor wants to list it. When you call, tell the realtor you want a low estimate of value so as to sell your home quickly and you want a long (detailed) copy of the data. Or say that you are not selling now, but want the unvarnished truth, a low estimate, because you may sell soon. Your object is to **obtain comparable sale prices lower than your property tax assessment. Ask for lowball 1990 comparables so you can see what property values have done in the past year.** Use the 1991 comparables to determine the value of your house for tax purposes. Or tell your realtor what your purpose, and that when you sell, you'll give him or her first crack at the listing.

You may be able to get this information by yourself. Real estate data are often kept on microfiche (condensed data on 5 by 8 inch film) at college campuses and libraries, at your assessor's office, government centers, and at many realtors' offices. Open the library property microfiche box. Regions usually start with Reg 1 (North) and go to Reg 3, 4, or 5 (South). Now find your **street.** It is listed alphanumerically. Look for your **house number,** and copy the data. Look up and down your street and nearby streets on the microfiche to find last year's (1990) sales, often listed in the upper righthand quadrant of the microfiche. You also can find your house listed alphabetically and by folio number. If you have time, look at the plat, which shows lot sizes clearly.

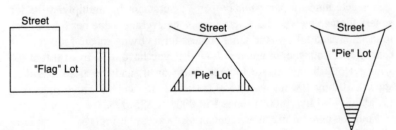

**Figure 3-1. Lots with Excess Footage Shaded.**

Recent sales books like *Real Estate Data Inc.* (REDI) are in many realtor's offices. Sales are classified geographically. Look in the subdivision index for the name of your neighborhood. The pages near your subdivision are the sales closest to your house, which are useful for developing comparables.

Most realty offices have computer terminals with various recent sales programs, such as **Recent Sales, Taxstar, Iscnet, Public Records Corp. (PRC),** and **Realtron.** The PRC-type program, like **Taxstar,** produces the comparables with the lowest mean (average) sales price. Why? Because this database includes foreclosure sales, auctions and for-sale-by-owner sales, whereas a Multi-Listing-Service (MLS) type database sometimes concentrates on higher-priced MLS (realtor/commission) sales. Thus a public records (PR) database is your best bet when you can get it. Some realtors are not familiar with the **PR,** but many are. They are most familiar with their MLS database of **recent sales,** and often with **PRC.** Give the realtor your folio number, the address of your house, and the legal address (it is on your proposed tax notice), because sometimes there are omissions and errors on the address listings. To simplify matters, you can photocopy your notice for the agent. Make sure the realtor uses a comparable sales database that includes foreclosures and auctions. Avoid using a high-price-skewed MLS-only database.

In an active market, an experienced realtor can forecast sales price and time on market with amazing accuracy; for example, $150,000 within 30 days, or $140,000 in a week. Houses selling for $300,000 or more are harder to predict because of the thinness of the market. Possible exceptions are the California, Washington, D.C., and New York areas, where prices are higher. By the same token, active markets are often rich in lowball comparables.

## *Live Ammo Versus Shooting Blanks*

**Live ammo is relevant comparable sales. Blanks are reasonable arguments unacceptable to the BofE.** Your object is to reduce your assessment, to establish a market value lower than your assessed value. Therefore, you look for sales of houses similar to and near to your house, but with lower sales prices (market value) than your house's assessed value. Auctioned houses in your area are a good source for lowball prices. Remember, **hard evidence is required, not hearsay.** You need **copies of the sale printouts, your ammunition,** or at least comparable information, as your assessor requires. You also need **signed copies of repair receipts**

**and estimates by licensed, bonded, and insured contractors.** At the hearing, the assessor has recent sales printouts to support his assessed value and he enjoys the presumption of correctness, until you overcome the presumption.

For example, if you say, "My neighbor, Mr. Y, at 10111 NW 67 Ave., **said** he bought his house for $80,000," you shoot blanks and destroy your credibility in a special master's eyes. Rare is the seller who doesn't add 10 percent to the actual price he received for his house, or the buyer who doesn't add or subtract thousands to impress his friends.

## Luck of the Draw

If you build a good case, you can often overcome any obstacle. The best-prepared adversary usually wins in this type of procedure. The oft-harried assessor may not be prepared. He knows he gets paid whether or not he wins your case. As many law school freshmen know, you can't count on the law being fair; there is an element of the crapshoot (chance, luck) in every judicial procedure. But **you can tilt chance in your favor.** The author, acting as a tax agent, recently obtained a $500,000 reduction on a shopping center for which the agent didn't deserve a dime's reduction. The special master was new, and her discernible dislike of the assessor enabled this tax agent (author) to play to this dissonance by depreciating the assessor comparables, while verbally enhancing his own (relatively poor) comparables and smiling a lot. It worked! Luck of the draw!

## Court System Quagmire

In a word, stay out of court. Lawyers are trained fighters. Their job is to turn hairline cracks into Grand Canyons. Priority drug and criminal cases have jammed court dockets to the point of near collapse in much of our state and federal judicial system. As a result, simple tax appeal civil cases, never a court priority, now often drag on for years.

The property tax petitioner plaintiff is made painfully aware of the lack of progress by monthly attorney billings at $100 to $400 per hour. And it is not unknown for a lawyer to prolong and complicate simple cases to increase billings. As a rule of thumb, only $3 million and up properties (those with a $75,000-plus tax bill) warrant attorney's fees, because the petitioner's personal time and legal expenses more than offset the potential reduction assessment of lesser properties. This is one reason that less than 1 percent of residential tax appeal cases get to court.

For example, if you are seeking a $50,000 tax assessment reduction, you may be looking at a $1,000 to $1,500 tax saving (20 to 30 mills times $50,000). But your legal fees will far exceed this amount.

## Learn Your State's Tax Appeal System

You may have a **state** appeals board that is superior to your local board, but inferior to a court appeal. Your state may require you to use this board before any court action.

If your state allows tax appeals to be argued in small claims court, use it! In this event, you can represent yourself, and informal rules of evidence apply. Usually, a small claims court is limited to compensation of less than $5,000. Judicial proceedings are often not prejudiced by prior tax appeal hearing results; you start with a clean slate. Deep clover!

By way of review, let's look at the average state judicial system sequence of events as it relates to your assessment petitions:

1. Get a prehearing conference to reduce your property taxes.

2. If not satisfied with your BofE, file an appeal to lower your property assessment with your BofE. Go to the BofE hearing and wait for the special master's notice that will be mailed to you.

3. If still not satisfied, appeal to your state tax appeals board, if you have one.

4. See if you can file a small claims court appeal. Represent yourself during this informal procedure; the formal rules of evidence are rarely used. This is often called "county court." But rarely is this court open to tax assessment petitioners. In some states you must file a complaint as a plaintiff in **circuit** (or **superior**) court after county court. You can represent yourself, but you must follow rules of evidence. You should have counsel.

5. Appeal circuit court decisions to the **district appellate court,** or superior court; appeal small claims court decisions to the circuit or superior court.

6. Appeal to your **state supreme court** as a last resort.

The federal court system is rarely involved, because property tax assessment is in the state's purview. State, not federal, issues are in question.

You only need to show the special master that a **preponderance of evidence** (or 51 percent probability) favors your tax assessment reduction petition. The **beyond-a-reasonable-doubt** principle (a probability more like 90 to 95 percent) applies to **criminal,** not **civil,** law.

*Don't forget your hearing appointment. BE THERE!*

"I forgot the appointment. Can you reschedule my case?" Almost always the answer is "No." No-shows forfeit their right to appeal. Consider your hearing notice written in stone, unless you have **very** powerful connections.

# 4

---

# *How to Build Your Tax Reduction Case*

Some terms used in this chapter: ''< ¼'' means **less than** one-quarter acre (Ac.). An acre is 43,560 square feet (sf), so this means the lot is less than 43,560/4 or < 10,890 sf. Use the actual sf if lot sizes vary more than 20 percent to 25 percent. The mean is the average. For example, the mean of 5, 10, and 20 is 35 divided by 3, or 11.67. REDI stands for Real Estate Data, Inc., a realtor book of recent sales. Microfiche, as explained earlier, is condensed property data stored on five by eight inch film, retrievable through a viewer that magnifies the script. Given: 90 percent or 0.9 CD.

The five numbered cases in this chapter show you how to build your case. First, find the microfiche, REDI sales data or computer printouts, scratchsheets, and final data sheet for each case. Then look at Case 1's microfiche printout and find the subject property. This is the source of information listed under the subject property column. Now find the comparables' data sheet or computer printout. It may be on the same page. This is where the sales information comes from for the columns of comparables that you find on the scratchsheet. Several cases have additional information, such as plats, maps, and other forms. If you have the time, adding such material can enhance your case by providing easy reference for the special master. If you get stuck, look at the answer form (the last page of each case). Then work backward toward the problem.

## Case 1, House: 1428 NE 10 St.—Single-Family Home

Peruse the following pages of an average appraisal. The only complicated procedure is the dollar adjustments to the subject in the "Sales Comparison Analysis" section on second page 40. Now look at the Sales and Subject Data page of the appraisal. The upper half of the page is REDI recent sales. The lower half is a microfiche tax roll printout that includes the subject. Cases 1, 2, and 3 are marked. By adding the land and improvement assessments, then dividing the sum into the taxes, you get the millage if there are no exemptions.

Look at the microfiche taxroll printout again. Find 1428 NE 10 St., the subject property. The assessor did not catch the house addition of a bedroom; he lists two bedrooms. But the appraiser noted three bedrooms during his inspection. Look at the exemption codes (H, V). H and V stand for Homestead and Veterans exemptions. The city, desiring military retirees, encourages vets by granting them a tax exemption. Find the folio number (10-7908-003-007) on the microfiche printout. Find the year the house was built (1955). Look at the column on the far right, at total assessed value or TV ($91,000), land value or LV ($18,000), and improvement value or IV, building ($72,000). Find the adj sq ft (1,783 sf) and Bed/Ba (2/1). Do you see where the assessor missed a bedroom? He lists a 3/1 on a 75 by 136 lot, which is 10,200 sf; it is in the legal in the lower left corner area. Because it is less than one-quarter acre, or less than 10,890 square feet, we use the symbol < ¼Ac. How much tax did the owner pay? (He paid $1,265.64.) For our example, use City of Miami-0101, a Miami tax district millage from Exhibit M. Exhibit M shows a Dade County, Florida, 1989 (rounded) millage range from 20 mills in Opalocka to 35 mills in Indian Creek, a 75 percent spread!

A word of tax explanation about the microfiche subject property printout. The $1,265 tax is a product of the Homestead millage times the assessed value, less the Homestead and Veteran exemptions, which vary. So the tax will be less than the millage times the assessed value. But the millage times the potential assessment reduction yields the potential tax dollars to be saved.

The owner of 1428 NE 10 St. had receipts for the following 1989 house repairs: **$5,000** for a roof estimate and a **$7,000** receipt for termite extermination and wood replacement. The owner couldn't afford the roof work, but the estimate is evidence that his house is less valuable nevertheless.

Look at 1428's REDI sales & subject data, on the upper half of the comp page. Find case 1. Find the yr blt, bed/ba, sale price, lot size. Sometimes

**Property Description & Analysis**  **UNIFORM RESIDENTIAL APPRAISAL REPORT**  **File No.**

| | | | |
|---|---|---|---|
| Property Address 1428 NE 10 St. (SW 309 st) | | Census Tract 110 | LENDER DISCRETIONARY USE |
| City Homestead  County Dade  State FL  Zip Code 33030 | | | Sale Price $ |
| Legal Description Sky Vista 2 Add PB 58-100 Lot/7 Blk 11 | | | Date |
| Owner/Occupant | Map Reference | | Mortgage Amount $ |
| Sale Price $ Refi  Date of Sale NA | PROPERTY RIGHTS APPRAISED | | Mortgage Type |
| Loan charges/concessions to be paid by seller $ Typical | XX Fee Simple | | Discount Points and Other Concessions |
| R.E. Taxes $ 718.36  Tax Year 1987  HOA $/Mo. 0 | ☐ Leasehold | | Paid by Seller $ |
| Lender/Client | ☐ Condominium (HUD/VA) | | |
| Fol 10 7908 008 007 | ☐ De Minimis PUD | | Source |

SUBJECT

| LOCATION | | ☐ Urban | X Suburban | ☐ Rural | NEIGHBORHOOD ANALYSIS | Good | Avg. | Fair | Poor |
|---|---|---|---|---|---|---|---|---|---|
| BUILT UP | (1) | XX Over 75% | ☐ 25-75% | ☐ Under 25% | Employment Stability | (1) X | | | |
| GROWTH RATE | | ☐ Rapid | X Stable | ☐ Slow | Convenience to Employment | | X | | |
| PROPERTY VALUES | | ☐ Increasing | X Stable | ☐ Declining | Convenience to Shopping | | X | | |
| DEMAND/SUPPLY | | ☐ Shortage | X In Balance | ☐ Over Supply | Convenience to Schools | | X | | |
| MARKETING TIME | | ☐ Under 3 Mos. | X 3-6 Mos. | ☐ Over 6 Mos. | Adequacy of Public Transportation | | X | | |

| PRESENT LAND USE | % | LAND USE CHANGE | PREDOMINANT | SINGLE FAMILY HOUSING | | Recreation Facilities | | X | | |
|---|---|---|---|---|---|---|---|---|---|---|
| Single Family | 90 | Not Likely X | OCCUPANCY | PRICE $ (000) | AGE (yrs) | Adequacy of Utilities | | X | | |
| 2-4 Family | | Likely | Owner 90% | | | Property Compatibility | | X | | |
| Multi-family | | In process | Tenant | 45 Low | | Protection from Detrimental Cond. | | X | | |
| Commercial | | To: | Vacant (0-5%) 5% | 90 High | | Police & Fire Protection | | X | | |
| Industrial | | | Vacant (over 5%) | Predominant | | General Appearance of Properties | | X | | |
| Vacant | 5 | | | 75 — 30 | | Appeal to Market | | X | | |

Note: Race or the racial composition of the neighborhood are not considered reliable appraisal factors.

COMMENTS: (1) This older neighborhood of mostly military retirees (subject is one) mixed with working class younger families is extremely stable

NEIGHBORHOOD

| Dimensions | 75 x 106 | | | Topography | Level |
|---|---|---|---|---|---|
| Site Area | 7950 sf | | | Size | Av |
| Zoning Classification | Single family | Corner Lot | No | Shape | Rectangular |
| HIGHEST & BEST USE: Present Use | Yes | Zoning Compliance | Yes | Drainage | Appears adequate |
| | | Other Use | No | View | Residential |

| UTILITIES | Public | Other | SITE IMPROVEMENTS | Type | Public | Private | Landscaping | Av |
|---|---|---|---|---|---|---|---|---|
| Electricity | X | | Street | Asphalt | X | | Driveway | Asphalt |
| Gas | | | Curb/Gutter | No | | | Apparent Easements | Rear alley (1) |
| Water | X | | Sidewalk | Yes | | | FEMA Flood Hazard Yes* x  No | |
| Sanitary Sewer | | Septic | Street Lights | " | X | | FEMA* Map/Zone 125098 0365 F 11/87 | |
| Storm Sewer | | | Alley | " | X | | | |

COMMENTS (Apparent adverse easements, encroachments, special assessments, slide areas, etc.): None with exception below
(1) Owner says 6' alley easement has been "ceded back" to him because waste pickup is now in front of house. It is still a utility easement.

SITE

| GENERAL DESCRIPTION | | EXTERIOR DESCRIPTION | | FOUNDATION | | BASEMENT | | INSULATION | |
|---|---|---|---|---|---|---|---|---|---|
| Units | 1 | Foundation | Unknown | Slab | Mammoth | Area Sq. Ft. 0 | | Roof | R19 X |
| Stories | 1 | Exterior Walls | CBS Stucco | Crawl Space | No | % Finished | | Ceiling | |
| Type (Det./Att.) | Det | Roof Surface | T & G | Basement | No | Ceiling | | Walls | Av |
| Design (Style) | Ran | Gutters & Dwnspts. | No | Sump Pump | No | Walls | | Floor | Av |
| Existing | Yes | Window Type | Al awning | Dampness | No | Floor | | None | |
| Proposed | No | Storm Sash | No | Settlement | No | Outside Entry | | Adequacy Av | |
| Under Construction | No | Screens | Yes | Infestation | No | | | Energy Efficient Items: | |
| Age (Yrs.) | 1955 | Manufactured House | No | | | | | 3½ ton A/C | |
| Effective Age (Yrs.) | 20 | | | | | | | | |

IMPROVEMENTS

| ROOMS | Foyer | Living | Dining | Kitchen | Den | Family Rm. | Rec. Rm. | Bedrooms | # Baths | Laundry | Other | Area Sq. Ft. |
|---|---|---|---|---|---|---|---|---|---|---|---|---|
| Basement | | | | | | | | | | | | |
| Level 1 | | 1 | Area | 1 | 1 | 1 | | 3 | 1 | | | 1764 |
| Level 2 | | | | | | | | | | | | |

Finished area above grade contains:  Rooms;  Bedroom(s);  Bath(s);  Square Feet of Gross Living Area

ROOM LIST

| SURFACES | Materials/Condition | HEATING | | KITCHEN EQUIP. | | ATTIC | | IMPROVEMENT ANALYSIS | Good | Avg. | Fair | Poor |
|---|---|---|---|---|---|---|---|---|---|---|---|---|
| Floors 30% tile ovr Terrazo; 35% ovr | | Type Rev/Cyc A/B | Refrigerator | X | None | | Quality of Construction | | X | | | |
| Walls opt ovr conc; 35% ovr | | Fuel Elec | Range/Oven | X | Stairs | | Condition of Improvements | | X | | | |
| Trim/Finish Wood / Terrazo | | Condition Av | Disposal | | Drop Stair | | Room Sizes/Layout | | X | | | |
| Bath Floor Terrazo | | Adequacy Av | Dishwasher | X | Scuttle | X | Closets and Storage | | X | | | |
| Bath Wainscot Yes | | COOLING | Fan/Hood | X | Floor | | Energy Efficiency | | X | | | |
| Doors Room: Wood | | Central Yes | Compactor | | Heated | | Plumbing-Adequacy & Condition | | X | | | |
| Closet: Bifolding Louvered | | Other No | Washer/Dryer | | Finished | | Electrical-Adequacy & Condition | | X | | | |
| Wood | | Condition Av | Microwave | X | truss | X | Kitchen Cabinets-Adequacy & Cond. | | X | | | |
| Fireplace(s) 0 # | | Adequacy Av | Intercom | | | | Compatibility to Neighborhood | | X | | | |

INTERIOR

| CAR STORAGE: | Garage | Attached | X | Adequate | | House Entry | X | Appeal & Marketability | | X | | |
|---|---|---|---|---|---|---|---|---|---|---|---|---|
| No. Cars 1 (3) | Carport X | Detached | | Inadequate | | Outside Entry | | Estimated Remaining Economic Life 30 | | | | Yrs. |
| Condition | None | Built-In | | Electric Door | | Basement Entry | X | Estimated Remaining Physical Life | | | | Yrs. |

AUTOS

Additional features: (1) Interior walls drywall. (2) Backup 150 amp system with solar source, ordinarily used for water heating (solar water heater). (3) Additional car space in driveway

Depreciation (Physical, functional and external inadequacies, repairs needed, modernization, etc.): An additional bathroom would be ideal, but not necessary as there are only two persons living there. No physical, functional or external inadequacies were noted. New upgraded kitchen and other minor improvements were noted.

General market conditions and prevalence and impact in subject/market area regarding loan discounts, interest buydowns and concessions: Good market conditions. No prevalence or impact in subject/market area regarding loan discounts, interest buydowns and concessions observed by appraisers on 4/22/88 and in previous appraisals in Homestead

COMMENTS

# UNIFORM RESIDENTIAL APPRAISAL REPORT

File No.

092-414/152 /03

Purpose of Appraisal is to estimate Market Value as defined in the Certification & Statement of Limiting Conditions.

## COST APPROACH

BUILDING SKETCH (SHOW GROSS LIVING AREA ABOVE GRADE)

If for Freddie Mac or Fannie Mae, show only square foot calculations and cost approach comments in this space.

```
              11
         Stor-
   16    age   11   15
         M Bed  Hall  Fam Rm
               Den
    42   Bedroo2  New   Dining
               Kit   Area      11
                             Work
         Bedroo3 Bath  Liv Rm  room
   NOT TO SCALE        42          20'
   42 X 42 = 1764 sq ft    Por  Car
                           14   port
```

ESTIMATED REPRODUCTION COST-NEW-OF IMPROVEMENTS:

| | | |
|---|---|---|
| Dwelling | Sq. Ft. @ $ | = $ |
| | Sq. Ft. @ $ | = $ |
| Extras | | = |
| | | = |
| Special Energy Efficient Items | | = |
| Porches, Patios, etc. | | = |
| Garage/Carport | Sq. Ft. @ $ | = |
| Total Estimated Cost New | | = $ |
| | Physical \| Functional \| External | |
| Less | | |
| Depreciation | | = $ |
| Depreciated Value of Improvements | | = $ |
| Site Imp. "as is" (driveway, landscaping, etc.) | | = $ |
| ESTIMATED SITE VALUE | | = $ 17,000 |
| (If leasehold, show only leasehold value.) | | |
| INDICATED VALUE BY COST APPROACH | | = $ |

(Not Required by Freddie Mac and Fannie Mae)

Does property conform to applicable HUD/VA property standards? ☐ Yes ☐ No

If No, explain:

Construction Warranty ☐ Yes ☒ No

Name of Warranty Program

Warranty Coverage Expires

## SALES COMPARISON ANALYSIS

The undersigned has recited three recent sales of properties most similar and proximate to subject and has considered these in the market analysis. The description includes a dollar adjustment, reflecting market reaction to those items of significant variation between the subject property and comparable properties. If a significant item in the comparable property is superior to, or more favorable than, the subject property, a minus (−) adjustment is made, thus reducing the indicated value of subject; if a significant item in the comparable is inferior to, or less favorable than, the subject property, a plus (+) adjustment is made, thus increasing the indicated value of the subject.

| ITEM | SUBJECT | COMPARABLE NO. 1 | | COMPARABLE NO. 2 | | COMPARABLE NO. 3 | |
|---|---|---|---|---|---|---|---|
| Address | 1428 NE 10 St (16480 SW 309 St) | 17220 SW 301 St | | 17300 SW 302 St | | 17270 SW 299 st | |
| Proximity to Subject | | .9 Mi WNW | | .9 Mi WNW | | .9 Mi WNW | |
| Sales Price | $ Refi | $ 69,000 | | $ 73,400 | | $ 76,700 | |
| Price/Gross Liv. Area | $ NA ☒ | $ 45.54 ☒ | | $ 48.04 ☒ | | $ 49.17 ☒ | |
| Data Source | Inspection, PR | REDI | | REDI | | REDI | |
| VALUE ADJUSTMENTS | DESCRIPTION | DESCRIPTION | + (−)$ Adjustment | DESCRIPTION | + (−)$ Adjustment | DESCRIPTION | + (−)$ Adjustment |
| Sales or Financing Concessions | | $69,000 Service Mtg | 3000 | None published | | None published | |
| Date of Sale/Time | NA | 10/87 (1) | | 2/88 | | 9/87 (1) | |
| Location | Dry/inside | Dry/inside | | Dry/inside | | Dry/inside | |
| Site/View | 7950sf/resid | 14382/residen | −6000 | 15255/reside | −7500 | 14382/residen | −600 |
| Design and Appeal | Ran/av | Ran/av | | Ran/av | | Ran/av | |
| Quality of Construction | CBS/av | CBS/av | | CBS/av | | CBS/av | |
| Age | 1955 | 1971 | | 1955 | | 1956 | |
| Condition | Av | Av | | Av | | Av−good | −4000 |
| Above Grade Room Count | Total 8 \| Bdrms 3 \| Baths 1 | Total Unk \| Bdrms 3 \| Baths 1 | | Total Unk \| Bdrms 3 \| Baths 2 | −1000 | Total Unk \| Bdrms 3 \| Baths 2 | −1000 |
| Gross Living Area | 1764 *meas Sq. Ft. | 3515 adj Sq. Ft. | 3500 | 1528 adj Sq. Ft. | 3500 | Sq. Ft. | 3000 |
| Basement & Finished Rooms Below Grade | 0 *1773adjØ | 0 | | 0 | | 0 | |
| Functional Utility | Av | Av | | Av | | Av | |
| Heating/Cooling | Cent A/C | Cent A/C | | Cent A/C | | Cent A/C | |
| Garage/Carport | 1-crpt + drvy | None | | None | | None | |
| Porches, Patio, Pools, etc. | Por, storeroom, workroom fen C/L | Al Sc Por − 1000 fen | | C/L fen | | C/L fen | |
| Special Energy Efficient Items | A/C 3½ Ton | Unknown | | Unk | | Unk | |
| Fireplace(s) | 0 | 0 | | 0 | | 0 | |
| Other (e.g. kitchen equip., remodeling) | Upgraded kit pkg | Unk | | Unk | | Unk | |
| Net Adj. (total) | | ☐ + ☐ − $ | | ☐ + ☐ − $ | | ☐ + ☐ − $ | |
| Indicated Value of Subject | | $ | | $ | | $ | |

Comments on Sales Comparison: (1) FNMA guidelines allow 12 month old comps; see Certifi. Addendum pp 2, 3 & 4. Comps 1 & 2 are superior to comp 3. Util $136 + maint $43 + Flood $19 + Haz $12 + tax $68 = $278/mo total

INDICATED VALUE BY SALES COMPARISON APPROACH ........................................................ $

INDICATED VALUE BY INCOME APPROACH (If Applicable) Estimated Market Rent $ 550 /Mo. x Gross Rent Multiplier = $ NA

This appraisal is made ☐ "as is" ☒ subject to the repairs, alterations, inspections or conditions listed below ☐ completion per plans and specifications.

Comments and Conditions of Appraisal:

## RECONCILIATION

Final Reconciliation:

This appraisal is based upon the above requirements, the certification, contingent and limiting conditions, and Market Value definition that are stated in

☐ FmHA, HUD &/or VA instructions.

☐ Freddie Mac Form 439 (Rev. 7/86)/Fannie Mae Form 1004B (Rev. 7/86) filed with client _____ 19 _____ ☐ attached.

I (WE) ESTIMATE THE MARKET VALUE, AS DEFINED, OF THE SUBJECT PROPERTY AS OF _____ 19 ___ to be $

I (We) certify: that to the best of my (our) knowledge and belief the facts and data used herein are true and correct; that I (we) personally inspected the subject property, both inside and out, and have made an exterior inspection of all comparable sales cited in this report; and that I (we) have no undisclosed interest, present or prospective therein.

Appraiser(s) SIGNATURE _____ NAME _____

Review Appraiser SIGNATURE _____ (if applicable) NAME _____

☐ Did ☐ Did Not Inspect Property

**Taxroll (from Microfiche)**
10-7908-003-007  TW 57 RG 39 SC 08 SUB 003 01-SINGLE FAMILY 01 SINGLE FAMILY
BLK - 11 LOT 7 MILI - 100 STATE USE - 01 87 - CON/PATIO    34 - C/L FENCE

|  |  |  |  |
|---|---|---|---|
| | 2 - CENT A/C T | | |
| | ADJ. SQ FT - 1,783 | | |
| 1428 NE 10 ST | BEDROOMS - 3 | $91,000 | - TV |
| HOMESTEAD, FL 33030 | BATHS - 1 | $18,000 | - LV |
| SKY VISTA 2ND ADDN PB 58-100 | YEAR BUILT - 1955 | $72,000 | - IV |
| LOT 7 BLK 11 LOT SIZE 75,000 X 136 | EXEMPT CODES - H,V | | |
| | | $1,265.64 | - TX |

**Comp #1**
FOLIO 30-7907-012-0052
SITUS     17220 SW 301 ST
          HOMESTEAD, FL 33030
BUYER: MCKENZIE, LYNN M.
SELLER: LEGGETT, RODNEY J.
MTG NAME: SERVICE MORTGAGE
          BLK 4 LOT 3
LEGAL - LT 3 BLK 4 PB 16/28
 *LAND USE - 01 SINGLE FAMILY
 *BDRMS - 3  *BATHS - 1
 *ADJ SQ FT - 1,515  *YEAR BUILT -71
  *PRIOR SALE - 03-73 $23,000   *EXTRA FEATURES - C/L FENCE,
  CENT A/C  ALUM STR

REC DT     10-87
SALES AMT      $69,000
MTG AMT        $69,000
STAMP AMT      $379.50
MTG TYPE: CNV
DEED TYPE: WD
BK/PG 13443-2829
LAND ASSMT      $9,810
IMPR ASSMT     $35,229
TAXES (85)     $399.95

**Comp #2**
FOLIO 30-7907-011-007
SITUS     17300 SW 302 ST
          HOMESTEAD, FL 33030
BUYER: WILKERSON, JAMES JR
SELLER: FARRELL, JOHN G.
          BLK 2 LOT 4
LEGAL - LTS 4 & 5 BLK 2 PB 26/46
 *LAND USE - 01 SINGLE FAMILY
 *BDRMS - 3   *BATHS - 2  *ADJ SQ FT - 1,528
 *PRIOR SALE - 11-78 $41,000

REC DT     2-88
SALE AMT        $73,400
STAMP AMT       $403.70
DEED TYPE: WD
BK/PG 13582-2312
LAND ASSMT      $17,780
IMPR ASSMT      $30,079
TAXES (85)      $446.24
          *YEAR BUILT - 55

**Comp #3**
FOLIO 30-7907-037-011
SITUS     17270 SW 299 ST
          HOMESTEAD, FL 33030
BUYER: STAUFFER, MILES I
SELLER: RICE, RICHARD L
          BLK 2 LOT 3
LEGAL - LT 3 BLK 2 PB 62/66
 *LAND USE - 01 SINGLE FAMILY
 *BDRMS - 3   *BATHS - 2   *ADJ SQ FT -1,560   *YEAR BUILT -56
 *PRIOR SALE - 05-84    *EXTRA FEATURES - C/L FENCE

REC DT     09-87
SALE AMT        $76,700
STAMP AMT       $421.85
DEED TYPE: WD
BK/PG 13400-2656
LAND ASSMT      $16,790
IMPR ASSMT      $31,501
TAXES (85)      $464.84

the lot size has to be determined by examining the plat, which is above the map. Using a pencil, transfer all relevant information onto the scratch-sheet. Look at the front, rear, and street scene of the subject and at the comp pictures. You don't absolutely need pictures, but they can help you at the hearing.

Now look at the bottom of the comp page, at the microfiche tax roll printout. Use the scratchsheet to record the data. Remember, you want sale prices lower than your house's assessed value, and the houses have to be similar to yours. Review the example in Chapter 3, Table 3-1. Questions to answer include:

- A. What is Miami 0101 millage?
- B. What is Case 1 total potential **assessment** reduction for repairs?
- C. Amount of **tax reduction** for repairs?

**MILLAGES APPLICABLE TO PROPERTY TAX ASSESSMENTS FOR 1989 TAX YEAR**

This cart shows in dollars and cents the amount paid to each taxing body for every $1,000 of assessed value. Refer to "Mill Code" shown on your Tax Bill and pick corresponding "Mill Code" on this chart to determine rates applicable. Where street lighting and improvement districts are involved, the code number identifying the district is shown on your Tax Bill.

| MILL CODE | MUNICIPALITIES OR COUNTY AREAS | SCHOOL OPERATING MILLAGE | SCH DEBT SVC | SOUTH FLORIDA WATER MANAGEMENT DIST. | FLORIDA INLAND NAVIGATION | CITY OPERATING MILLAGE | DEBT SVC. | MISC. MILLAGE ON NON-EXEMPT VALUE ONLY | COUNTYWIDE | DEBT SVC | UNINCORPORATED MUNICIPAL SERVICE AREA | FIRE AND RESCUE | LIBRARY MILLAGE | LIBRARY VOTED DEBT | SPECIAL ASSESSMENT INSTALLMENT ON IMP. DIST | 1989 TOTAL MILLAGE | 1988 TOTAL MILLAGE |
|---|---|---|---|---|---|---|---|---|---|---|---|---|---|---|---|---|---|
| 0100 | Miami | 8.190 | 0.359 | .547 | .0370 | 9.5995 | 2.3381 | | 7.095 | 1.294 | | | .459 | .500 | | 30.4186 | 29.7241 |
| 0101 | Miami | 8.190 | 0.359 | .547 | .0370 | 9.5995 | 2.3381 | 0.500 | 7.095 | 1.294 | | | .459 | .500 | | 30.9186 | 30.2241 |
| 0101 | Miami | 8.190 | 0.359 | .547 | .0370 | 9.5995 | | | 7.095 | 1.294 | | | .459 | .500 | | 32.1520 | 31.4575 |
| 0300 | Coral Gables | 8.190 | 0.359 | .547 | .0370 | 4.8890 | 0.1920 | | 7.095 | 1.294 | | | .459 | .500 | | 23.5620 | 23.2425 |
| 0400 | Hialeah | 8.190 | 0.359 | .547 | .0370 | 7.4380 | | 0.342 | 7.095 | 1.294 | | | | | | 25.3020 | 24.8365 |
| 0500 | Miami Springs | 8.190 | 0.359 | .547 | .0370 | 5.9500 | | | 7.095 | 1.294 | | 2.446 | .459 | .500 | | 25.8770 | 25.2835 |
| 0600 | North Miami | 8.190 | 0.359 | .547 | .0370 | 6.6910 | | | 7.095 | 1.294 | | 2.446 | | | | 26.6590 | 25.7155 |
| 0601 | North Miami | 8.190 | 0.359 | .547 | .0370 | 6.6910 | | 0.962 | 7.095 | 1.294 | | 2.446 | | | | 27.6210 | 26.7025 |
| 0604 | North Miami | 8.190 | 0.359 | .547 | .0370 | 6.6910 | | 0.962 | 7.095 | 1.294 | | 2.446 | | | X | 27.6210 | 26.7025 |
| 0700 | No. Miami Beach | 8.190 | 0.359 | .547 | .0370 | 8.1200 | | | 7.095 | 1.294 | | 2.446 | | | | 28.0880 | 25.9945 |
| 0701 | No. Miami Beach | 8.190 | 0.359 | .547 | .0370 | | | | 7.095 | 1.294 | | 2.446 | | | | 19.9680 | 19.1735 |
| 0800 | Opa-locka | 8.190 | 0.359 | .547 | .0370 | 9.3000 | 0.4610 | | 7.095 | 1.294 | | 2.446 | | | | 29.7290 | 28.9265 |
| 0801 | Opa-locka | 8.190 | 0.359 | .547 | .0370 | | | | 7.095 | 1.294 | | 2.446 | | | | 19.9680 | 19.1735 |
| 0900 | South Miami | 8.190 | 0.359 | .547 | .0370 | 6.0800 | | | 7.095 | 1.294 | | 2.446 | .459 | .500 | | 27.0070 | 26.0735 |
| 0901 | South Miami | 8.190 | 0.359 | .547 | .0370 | 6.0800 | | | 7.095 | 1.294 | | 2.446 | .459 | .500 | X | 27.0070 | 26.0735 |
| 1000 | Homestead | 8.190 | 0.359 | .547 | .0370 | 8.4533 | | | 7.095 | 1.294 | | 2.446 | .459 | .500 | | 29.3803 | 28.5551 |
| 1002 | Homestead | 8.190 | 0.359 | .547 | .0370 | 8.4533 | | | 7.095 | 1.294 | | 2.446 | .459 | .500 | X | 29.3803 | 28.5551 |
| 1100 | Miami Shores | 8.190 | 0.359 | .547 | .0370 | 8.3800 | | | 7.095 | 1.294 | | 2.446 | | | | 28.3480 | 26.5535 |
| 1200 | Bal Harbour | 8.190 | 0.359 | .547 | .0370 | 3.6000 | | | 7.095 | 1.294 | | 2.446 | | | | 23.5680 | 22.9535 |
| 1300 | Bay Harbour Isl. | 8.190 | 0.359 | .547 | .0370 | 3.9760 | | | 7.095 | 1.294 | | 2.446 | | | | 23.9440 | 22.7255 |
| 1400 | Surfside | 8.190 | 0.359 | .547 | .0370 | 5.8600 | | | 7.095 | 1.294 | | 2.446 | | | | 25.8280 | 24.5342 |
| 1500 | West Miami | 8.190 | 0.359 | .547 | .0370 | 5.2500 | | | 7.095 | 1.294 | | 2.446 | .459 | .500 | | 26.1170 | 25.0735 |
| 1600 | Florida City | 8.190 | 0.359 | .547 | .0370 | 6.3000 | | | 7.095 | 1.294 | | 2.446 | .459 | .500 | | 27.2270 | 25.6645 |
| 1700 | Biscayne Park | 8.190 | 0.359 | .547 | .0370 | 5.0000 | | | 7.095 | 1.294 | | 2.446 | .459 | .500 | | 25.9270 | 24.5635 |
| 1800 | El Portal | 8.190 | 0.359 | .547 | .0370 | 7.3220 | | | 7.095 | 1.294 | | 2.446 | .459 | .500 | | 28.2490 | 27.4615 |
| 1900 | Golden Beach | 8.190 | 0.359 | .547 | .0370 | 8.8356 | | | 7.095 | 1.294 | | 2.446 | .459 | .500 | | 29.7826 | 29.9091 |
| 2100 | Indian Creek | 8.190 | 0.359 | .547 | .0370 | 10.0000 | | 4.200 | 7.095 | 1.294 | | 2.446 | .459 | .500 | | 35.1270 | 34.2735 |
| 2200 | Medley | 8.190 | 0.359 | .547 | .0370 | 7.7710 | 0.2000 | | 7.095 | 1.294 | | 2.446 | .459 | .500 | | 28.8980 | 28.0445 |
| 2201 | Medley | 8.190 | 0.359 | .547 | .0370 | 7.7710 | 0.2000 | | 7.095 | 1.294 | | 2.446 | .459 | .500 | X | 28.8980 | 28.0445 |
| 2300 | N. Bay Village | 8.190 | 0.359 | .547 | .0370 | 4.2790 | 0.7820 | | 7.095 | 1.294 | | 2.446 | .459 | .500 | | 25.9880 | 25.1345 |
| 2500 | Sweetwater | 8.190 | 0.359 | .547 | .0370 | 2.9900 | | | 7.095 | 1.294 | | 2.446 | .459 | .500 | | 23.9170 | 23.1035 |
| 2600 | Virginia Gardens | 8.190 | 0.359 | .547 | .0370 | 2.0000 | | | 7.095 | 1.294 | | 2.446 | .459 | .500 | | 26.7070 | 25.8595 |
| 2701 | Hialeah Gardens | 8.190 | 0.359 | .547 | .0370 | 5.7800 | | | 7.095 | 1.294 | | 2.446 | .459 | .500 | X | 26.7070 | 25.8595 |
| 2900 | Islandia | 8.190 | 0.359 | .547 | .0370 | 10.0000 | | | 7.095 | 1.294 | | | .459 | .500 | | 28.4810 | 27.7865 |
| 3000 | County | 8.190 | 0.359 | .547 | .0370 | | | | 7.095 | 1.294 | | 2.446 | .459 | .500 | | 23.2540 | 23.1415 |
| 3001 | County | 8.190 | 0.359 | .547 | .0370 | | | | 7.095 | 1.294 | 2.327 | 2.446 | .459 | .500 | X | 23.2540 | 23.1415 |
| 3002 | County | 8.190 | 0.359 | .547 | .0370 | | | | 7.095 | 1.294 | 2.327 | 2.446 | .459 | .500 | X | 23.2540 | 23.1415 |
| 3003 | County | 8.190 | 0.359 | .547 | .0370 | | | | 7.095 | 1.294 | 2.327 | 2.446 | .459 | .500 | X | 23.2540 | 23.1415 |
| 3004 | County | 8.190 | 0.359 | .547 | .0370 | | | | 7.095 | 1.294 | 2.327 | 2.446 | .459 | .500 | X X | 23.2540 | 23.1415 |
| 3005 | County | 8.190 | 0.359 | .547 | .0370 | | | | 7.095 | 1.294 | 2.327 | 2.446 | .459 | .500 | X X | 23.2540 | 23.1415 |

D. What is the total potential reduction from the **sales comparison analysis?**

E. What is the total repairs plus sales analysis reduction?

Find the 1989 millage from Exhibit A, $.0309186, which is 30.918 mills. Multiply the millage times the total proposed reduction, $12,000, plus the $16,737 assessment reduction (see bottom of page 44) to obtain $889 tax dollars saved ($.0309186 × $28,737 = $889).

---

**Case 1.  TAX REDUCTION DATA Scratchsheet.**

|  | **Subject** | **Comp 1** | **Comp 2** | **Comp 3** |
|---|---|---|---|---|
| **Address** | _____ | _____ | _____ | _____ |
| **Sales price** | _____[1] | _____ | _____ | _____ |
| **Sq ft**[2] | _____ | _____ | _____ | _____ |
| **$___/sf** | _____ | _____ | _____ | _____ |
| **Lot size** | _____ | _____ | _____ | _____ |
| **Sale date**[3] | _____ | _____ | _____ | _____ |
| **Bd/Ba** | _____ | _____ | _____ | _____ |
| **Dist from subj** | 0 | _____ | _____ | _____ |
| **Yr blt** | 19_____ | 19_____ | 19_____ | 19_____ |

Mean$/sf[4] = $_____    ÷3 ×[Subj sf] × $0.9^5$ = $_____    proper value. $_____
less $_____  = $_____    assessment reduction × .0_____    [mills] = $_____
tax saving from sales analysis and/or home repairs.

[1] $_____ is the county assessed value, not the sales price.
[2] Either adj or liv sf, but not both.
[3] The comparable sales must have occurred in the 12 months before 1/1/89.
[4] Mean = [Comp 1 $/sf + Comp 2 + Comp 3] ÷ 3.
[5] You can deduct 10 percent of the sales price as sales expense.

---

## Answers to Case 1 Questions

A. City of Miami millage code 0101 is 30,9186.
B. Total potential assessment reduction for repairs: $5,000 for roof plus $7,000 for termites equals $12,000 potential assessment reduction.
C. Tax Reduction for repairs = $12,000 times 30.9188 mills equals $371.00 tax reduction.
D. Total potential reduction from sales comparison analysis.1988 house repair receipts & estimate = $.0309186 × [$7,000 + $5,000] = $371.
E. $518 + $371 = **889 total dollars saved from repairs & sales analysis.**

---

### Case 1.  TAX REDUCTION DATA.

|  | Subject | Comp 1 | Comp 2 | Comp 3 |
|---|---|---|---|---|
| **Address** | 1428 NE 10 St. | 17220 SW 301 | 17300 SW 302 | 17270 SW 299 |
| **Sales price** | $91,000[1] | $69,000 | $73,400 | $76,700 |
| **Sq ft[2]** | 1,783 | 1,515 | 1,528 | 1,560 |
| **$___/sf** | $51.04/sf | $44.22/sf | $46.73/sf | $47.88/sf |
| **Lot size** | < ¼Ac | < ¼Ac | < ¼Ac | < ¼Ac |
| **Sale date[3]** | NA | 10/87 | 2/88 | 9/87 |
| **Bd/Ba** | 3/1 | 3/1 | 3/2 (−$2,000) | 3/2 (−$2,000) |
| **Dist from subj** | 0 | 0.9 mi WNW | 0.9 mi WNW | 0.9 mi WNW |
| **Yr blt** | 1955 | 1971 | 1955 | 1956 |

---

Hint: Take the three comp sales prices; subtract $2,000 for the 2nd bath from each comp; average the $/sqft. Multiply by your house's sqft to get proper market (in contrast to assessed) value. For example, the avg $/sqft (of the best 3 comps) is $46.28 × subject 1,783 sf = $82,514 proper market value (less repairs). City of Miami (code 0101) millage = 30.9188. Mean $/sf[4] = $46.28 × 1,783 [Subj sf] × 0.9[5] = $74,262 proper value. $91,000 − $74,262 = $16,737 assessment reduction × .0309186 [mills] = $518 tax saving from sales comparison analysis.

[1] Here, subject **$91,000 is the county assessed value,** not the sales price.
[2] Sq ft: liv or adj, but not both in same case.

[3] The comparable sales should have occurred in 1988.

[4] X$/sf = [Comp 1 $/sf + Comp 2 $/sf + Comp 3 $/sf] ÷ 3 = $46.28. Remember to take off $2,000 from the sales prices before dividing by the house's square footage.

[5] 0.9 = the CD, here equal to the 10 percent sales costs deduction.

---

## Case 2, House: 912 NW 179 St.—Single-Family Home

This case is similar to Case 1, but omits peripheral material. The appraiser report summarizes the raw data found below. The appraiser report data may vary somewhat from your answer sheet (i.e., in square footage). We are using adjusted square feet throughout Case 2.

Look at the subject property data in the **Taxstar** program printout. In July 1981 the house sold for $55,000. The comparables are on the REDI sales summary page, arranged by subdivision name and by folio number. We have placed the three cases on one page, for ease of reference. Look at the other data. Find the comparables on the REDI recent sales page excerpt. Determine the amount of the potential reduction from the sales analysis scratchsheet below. Use the 1989 county millage code 3000 from Exhibit A. What is the comparative sales analysis potential reduction in saved tax dollars? (The completed datasheet shows that it is $249.) Completed Tax Reduction Data appears at the end of Case 2.

Purpose of Appraisal is to estimate Market Value as defined in the Certification & Statement of Limiting Conditions.

## COST APPROACH

| BUILDING SKETCH (SHOW GROSS LIVING AREA ABOVE GRADE) If for Freddie Mac or Fannie Mae, show only square foot calculations and cost approach comments in this space. | ESTIMATED REPRODUCTION COST – NEW – OF IMPROVEMENTS: |
|---|---|

ESTIMATED REPRODUCTION COST – NEW – OF IMPROVEMENTS:

Dwelling _____ Sq. Ft. @ $ _____ = $ _____
_____ Sq. Ft. @ $ _____ = _____
Extras _____ = _____
_____ = _____
Special Energy Efficient Items _____ = _____
Porches, Patios, etc. _____ = _____
Garage/Carport _____ Sq. Ft. @ $ _____ = _____
Total Estimated Cost New ..................... = $ _____

|  | Physical | Functional | External |
|---|---|---|---|
| Less | | | |

Depreciation _____ = $ _____
Depreciated Value of Improvements ............. = $ _____
Site Imp. "as is" (driveway, landscaping, etc.) = $ _____
ESTIMATED SITE VALUE ............................. = $ 20,000
(If leasehold, show only leasehold value.)
INDICATED VALUE BY COST APPROACH ........ = $ _____

$$(25 \times 48) + (8 \times 3) = 1,251 \text{ liv sq ft}$$

(Not Required by Freddie Mac and Fannie Mae)
Does property conform to applicable HUD/VA property standards?  [X] Yes  [ ] No
If No, explain: _____

Construction Warranty  [ ] Yes  [X] No
Name of Warranty Program _____
Warranty Coverage Expires _____

## SALES COMPARISON ANALYSIS

The undersigned has recited three recent sales of properties most similar and proximate to subject and has considered these in the market analysis. The description includes a dollar adjustment, reflecting market reaction to those items of significant variation between the subject and comparable properties. If a significant item in the comparable property is superior to, or more favorable than, the subject property, a minus (–) adjustment is made, thus reducing the indicated value of subject; if a significant item in the comparable is inferior to, or less favorable than, the subject property, a plus (+) adjustment is made, thus increasing the indicated value of the subject.

| ITEM | SUBJECT | COMPARABLE NO. 1 | | COMPARABLE NO. 2 | | COMPARABLE NO. 3 | |
|---|---|---|---|---|---|---|---|
| Address | 912 NW 179 st | 700 NW 179 St | | 17501 NW Sunshine St Pkwy | | 18130 NW 8 Pl | |
| Proximity to Subject | | 1½ Blocks E | | 1½ Blocks SSE | | 1½ Blocks N | |
| Sales Price | $67,000 | | $ 62,900 | | $ 63,000 | | $ 62,000 |
| Price/Gross Liv. Area | $ 53.56 ☑ | $ 49.33 ☑ | | $ 47.37 ☑ | | $ 48.36 ☑ | |
| Data Source | REDI, Taxstar | REDI, Taxstar | | REDI, Taxstar | | REDI, Taxstar | |
| VALUE ADJUSTMENTS | DESCRIPTION | DESCRIPTION | + (–) $ Adjustment | DESCRIPTION | + (–) $ Adjustment | DESCRIPTION | + (–) $ Adjustment |
| Sales or Financing Concessions | | $64,459 FHA Statewide Mtg | | $63,500 FHA Fed Mtg Assoc | | $62,500 CNV Citicorp Sav | 500 |
| Date of Sale/Time | 2/88 Proposal | 10/88 | | 11/88 | | 9/88 | |
| Location | Inside | Cor | 1500 | Inside | 1500 | Inside (3) | 1500 |
| Site/View | 80250/Reside | 95400/Resid | –1000 | 80000/Resid | | 868600/Resid | |
| Design and Appeal | Ranch/Av | Ranch/Av | | Ranch/Av | | Clone of Subj | |
| Quality of Construction | Av | Av | | Av | | Av | |
| Age | 1957 | 1958 | | 1959 | | 1955 | |
| Condition | Av + 2 year old roof | Av (5) | 3000 | Av (5) | | Av (5) | 3000 |
| Above Grade Room Count | 6 : 4 : 1 | 5 : 3 : 2 | –2000 | 5 : 3 : 1 | | 5 : 3 : 1 | |
| Gross Living Area | 1251 Sq. Ft. | 1275 Sq. Ft. | | 1330 Sq. Ft. | | 1282 Sq. Ft. | |
| Basement & Finished Rooms Below Grade | 1251/1295 adj Ø = .97 | 1314 adj Ø x .97 = 1275 Ø | | 1371 adjØ x .97 = 1330 Ø | | 1322 adj Ø x .97 = 1282 Ø | |
| Functional Utility | Av | Av | | Av | | Av | |
| Heating/Cooling | Wall | Wall | | Wall | | None observed in Front | |
| Garage/Carport | 0 | 0 | | Carport | | Garage (4) | –3000 |
| Porches, Patio, Pools, etc. | Rear patio | Similar | | Similar | | Similar | |
| Special Energy Efficient Items | None | None | | None | | None | |
| Fireplace(s) | 0 | 0 | | 0 | | 0 | |
| Other (e.g. kitchen equip., remodeling) | Remodelled 1986 | Appears to be remodelled (4) | | Appears to be remodelled (4) | | Appears to be remodelled (4) | |
| Net Adj. (total) | | [X] + [ ] – $ | 1500 | [X] + [ ] – $ | 2000 | [X] + [ ] – $ | 2000 |
| Indicated Value of Subject | | | $ 64,400 | | $ 65,000 | | $ 64,000 |

Comments on Sales Comparison: (1) Faces N/S Section Rd traffic artery. (2) faces Fl Tpk; (3) Across St from Shopping Center. (4) External inspection only. Comps equally weighted (5) Rudy Martinez, Duran Roofing Inc Lic #00016156, bonded ins etc. says, "$3,000 is about right."

INDICATED VALUE BY SALES COMPARISON APPROACH ..................................................... $ _____
INDICATED VALUE BY INCOME APPROACH (If Applicable) Estimated Market Rent $ 550 /Mo. x Gross Rent Multiplier NA = $ NA
This appraisal is made [ ] "as is" [X] subject to the repairs, alterations, inspections or conditions listed below [ ] completion per plans and specifications.
Comments and Conditions of Appraisal: Estimated closing costs: $2050. Util 87; Maintenance $34. Flood ins $19. Haz ins $13. Tax $66. Total "monthly expenses" $219. VC-1 required. Conforms to society, **
Final Reconciliation: Sales Comparison Approach is sole criterion of value

## RECONCILIATION

**institute norms

This appraisal is based upon the above requirements, the certification, contingent and limiting conditions, and Market Value definition that are stated in
[X] FmHA, HUD &/or VA instructions.
[ ] Freddie Mac Form 439 (Rev. 7/86)/Fannie Mae Form 1004B (Rev. 7/86) filed with client _____ 19 _____  [ ] attached.
I (WE) ESTIMATE THE MARKET VALUE, AS DEFINED, OF THE SUBJECT PROPERTY AS OF _____ 19 _____ to be $ _____

I (We) certify: that to the best of my (our) knowledge and belief the facts and data used herein are true and correct; that I (we) personally inspected the subject property, both inside and out, and have made an exterior inspection of all comparable sales cited in this report; and that I (we) have no undisclosed interest, present or prospective therein.

Appraiser(s) SIGNATURE _____
NAME _____

Review Appraiser SIGNATURE _____
(if applicable) NAME _____
[ ] Did [ ] Did Not Inspect Property

Freddie Mac Form 70 10/86  **12Ch.**    Forms and Worms Inc.,® 315 Whitney Ave., New Haven, CT 06511  1(800) 243-4545    Fannie Mae Form 1004 10/86

## TAXSTAR PROGRAM PRINTOUT

DCR REPORT
FOLIO : 30-21-11-004-0190
CO-USE: RESID-SINGLE FA ( 1)
ZONING: 100          SALE DT: SE/86

ADDR: 912 NW 179TH ST
SUBDV: SCOTT LAKE MANOR SEC 2
PRICE : $ 0          CHANGE DATE: 07/JA/89

OWNER NAME & ADDRESS

LAND & PROPERTY DESCRIPTION
FRONT: 0          DEPTH: 0          LAND SIZE: 0          (ACRES) LOT: 4          BLK: 9
STATE-USE: RESID-SINGLE FAMI ( 1) ZONING:          LOT SIZE: 75 X107
TAX YEAR 1988

| LAND-VAL: $ 32,898 | TOTAL VALUE | BEDROOMS : 4 | YR-BUILT : 1957 |
| IMPR-VAL: $ 44,894 | 67792 | BATHROOMS: 1 | ADJ-SQ FT: 1295 |

EXTRA FEATURES
C/L FENCE 4'          (034)  PATIO/SLAB (CONCRETE 087)          STORAGE SHED          (122)

SALES HISTORY

| DEED DATE | PRICE | TYPE | OR BOOK-PAGE | OWNER NAME |
|-----------|-------|------|--------------|------------|
| CURR: SE/86 | $    0 | 5 | 13153–00636 | VOSS NORMA JEAN |
| PREV: JN/86 | $    0 | 3 | 12946–01317 | |
| EARL: JL/81 | $ 55000 | 1 | 11167–01597 | |

TAXES $ ASSESSMENT INFORMATION

| ASSESSED VALUE (1989) | DISTRICT | EXEMPTIONS | AUTHORITY/TAX AMOUNT (1988) | |
|-----------------------|----------|------------|------------------|------|
| LAND :  $  32,898 | | | COUNTY   TAX:$ | 1737 |
| IMPRV: $  44,894 | | | CITY         TAX:$ | 0 |
| TOTAL: $  67,792 | | | OTHER      TAX:$ | 381 |
| PREV:  $  67,792 | | | GROSS     TAX:$ | 2119 |

TOT-MILL RATE: 0.0231415  EXEMPT AMT: $0.00          NON-EX AMT: $          67792

LEGAL DESCRIPTION
LEGAL :    SCOTT LAKE MANOR SEC 2          PB 60-58
               LOT 4 BLK 9          LOT SIZE SITE VALUE
               OR 13153-636 0986 5          OR 12946-1317 0686 3

**Comp #1**

| | |
|---|---|
| FOLIO 30-2111-009-001 | REC DT    10-88 |
| SITUS      700 NW 179 ST | SALES AMT                 $62,900 |
|                MIAMI FL 33169 | MTG AMT                     $64,459 |
| BUYER: HENRY, CLIFFORD N. | STAMP AMT                  $345.95 |
| SELLER: WALFISH, ROSALIE R. | MTG TYPE: FHA |
| MTG NAME: STATE WIDE MTG CORP | DEED TYPE: WD |
|                BLK 1 LOT 1 | BK/PG 13845-69 |
| LAND USE - SINGLE FAMILY | LAND ASSMT                $15,500 |
|   *BATHS - 2 | IMPR ASSMT                $26,167 |
|   *BDRMS - 3 | TAXES (85)                  $609.53 |
|   *YEAR BUILT - 58 | *ADJ SQ FT - 1,314 |
| LEGAL - LT 1 BLL 1 PB 65/114 | 90 X 106 |

**Comp #2**

| | |
|---|---|
| FOLIO 30-2111-009-093 | REC DT    10-88 |
| SITUS      17501 NW SUNSHINE STATE PKWY | SALE AMT                    $63,000 |
|                MIAMI FL 33169 | MTG AMT                     $63,500 |
| BUYER: OGLESBY, BILLY D. | STAMP AMT                  $324.50 |
| SELLER; MADISON, CAROLE | MTG TYPE: FHA |
| MTG NAME: FEDERATED MORTGAGE ASSOC | DEED TYPE: WD |
|                BLK 5 LOT 18 | BK/PG 13866-2744 |
|   *LAND USE - SINGLE FAMILY | LAND ASSMT                $14,442 |
|   *BATHS - 1 | IMPR ASSMT                $29,080 |
|   *BDRMS - 3 | TAXES (85)                  $640.34 |
|   *YEAR BUILT - 59 | *CENT A/C T |
| LEGAL - LT 18 BLK 5 PB 65/114 | *ADJ SQ FT - 1,371 |
| | 80 X 100+ |

**Comp #3**

| | |
|---|---|
| FOLIO 30-2111-003-060 | REC DT    09-88 |
| SITUS      18130 NW 8 PL | SALE AMT                    $62,000 |
| BUYER: AUDIGE, ARMAND | MTG AMT                     $46,500 |
| SELLER: IEN, DOROTHY | STAMP AMT                  $346.50 |
| MTG NAME: CITICORP SAVINGS FL | MTG TYPE: CNV |
|   *LAND USE: SINGLE FAMILY | DEED TYPE: WD |
|   *PRIOR SALE - $42,000 03-81 | BK/PG 13829-3420 |
|   *BATHS - 1 | LAND ASSMT                $14,442 |
|   *BDRMS - 3 | IMPR ASSMT                $25,354 |
|   *YEAR BUILT - 59 | TAXES (85)               $1,057.58 |
| LEGAL - LT 4 BLK 5 PB 57/79 | *ADJ SQ FT - 1,322 |
| | 86 X 101 |

**Case 2.  TAX REDUCTION DATA Scratchsheet.**

| | Subject | Comp 1 | Comp 2 | Comp 3 |
|---|---|---|---|---|
| Address | _____ | _____ | _____ | _____ |
| Sales price | _____[1] | _____ | _____ | _____ |
| Sq ft[2] | _____ | _____ | _____ | _____ |
| $__/sf | _____ | _____ | _____ | _____ |
| Lot size | _____ | _____ | _____ | _____ |
| Sale date[3] | _____ | _____ | _____ | _____ |
| Bd/Ba | _____ | _____ | _____ | _____ |
| Dist from subj | 0 | _____ | _____ | _____ |
| Yr blt | 19_____ | 19_____ | 19_____ | 19_____ |

Mean$/sf [4] = \$_____   ÷3 ×   [Subj sf] × $0.9^5$ = \$_____   proper value. \$_____
less \$_____   = \$_____   assessment reduction × .0_____   [mills] = \$_____
tax saving from sales analysis and/or home repairs.

[1] \$_____ is the county assessed value, not the sales price.
[2] Either adj or liv sf, but not both.
[3] The comparable sales must have occurred in the 12 months before 1/1/89.
[4] Mean = [Comp 1 $/sf + Comp 2 + Comp 3] ÷ 3.
[5] You can deduct 10 percent of the sales price as sales expense.

## Case 2.  TAX REDUCTION DATA.

|  | Subject | Comp 1 | Comp 2 | Comp 3 |
|---|---|---|---|---|
| **Address** | 912 NW 179 St | 700 NW 179 | 17501 NW Sunshine | 18130 NW 8 |
| **Sales price** | $67,792[1] | $62,900 | $63,000 | $62,000 |
| **Sq ft**[2] | 1,295 | 1,314 | 1,371 | 1,322 |
| **$__/sf** | $67.25/sf | $46.35/sf[3] | $45.95/sf | $46.90/sf |
| **Lot size** | < ¼Ac | < ¼Ac | < ¼Ac | < ¼Ac |
| **Sale date**[4] | NA | 10/88 | 11/88 | 9/88 |
| **Bd/Ba** | 4/1[5] | 3/2 (−$2,000) | 3/1 | 3/1 |
| **Dist from subj** | 0 | 2 blks E | 2 blks SSE | 2 blks N |
| **Yr blt** | 1957 | 1958 | 1959 | 1955 |

**County millage = 23.2540. Mean $/sf = $46.40**[6] × 1,295 [Subj sf] × 0.9[7] [CD, equal here to 10 percent deductible sales costs] = $54,078 proper assessed value. Taxstar printout assessed total value is $67,792, less $54,078 = $10,714 overassessment × $0.023254 (23.254 mills) = **$249 potential tax dollars saved from comparative sales analysis.**

[1] Subject $67,792 is the county assessed value, not a sale.
[2] Either adj sf or liv sf, but not both.
[3] $62,900 − $2,000 (extra bathroom) = $60,900/1,314 sf = $46.35/sf.
[4] Must be 1988 sales for 1989 tax year; assume they are.
[5] Three- and four-bedroom houses may be treated as three bedrooms.
[6] [$46.35 + $45.95 + $46.90] ÷ 3 = $46.40.
[7] CD of 0.9, or 90 percent, equal to 10 percent of the sales price as sales expense.

## *Subject 3: 5700 Grenada—Expensive Single-Family Home*

Fewer than 2 percent of house purchases exceed $250,000, so the market is usually a tougher sell. Look at the photocopy of the county records house sketch on page 2 of the appraisal report, upper left corner. Most assessors have similar data. The comp microfiche data and REDI comp data are condensed on the next page. It is 23.5620.

**Valuation Section**

Purpose of Appraisal is to estimate Market Value as defined in the Certification & Statement of Limiting Conditions.

**COST APPROACH**

| BUILDING SKETCH (SHOW GROSS LIVING AREA ABOVE GRADE) If for Freddie Mac or Fannie Mae, show only square foot calculations and cost approach comments in this space. | | |
|---|---|---|

**ESTIMATED REPRODUCTION COST – NEW – OF IMPROVEMENTS:**

| | | | |
|---|---|---|---|
| Dwelling 5469 | Sq. Ft. @ $ 42 | = $ | 213 |
| | Sq. Ft. @ $ | | |
| Extras Boathouse 60 x 20 | | = | 40~ |
| Elec driveway gates, fen | | = | 30 |
| Special Energy Efficient Items | | = | |
| Porches, Patios, etc. Pool | | = | 80 |
| Garage/Carport 1150 Sq. Ft. @ $ 19 | | = | 22 |
| Total Estimated Cost New | | = $ | 385 |

| | Physical | Functional | External |
|---|---|---|---|
| Less Depreciation | 50 | 50 | |

| | | |
|---|---|---|
| | = $ | (100) |
| Depreciated Value of Improvements | = $ | 285 |
| Site Imp. "as is" (driveway, landscaping, etc.) | = $ | 150 |
| ESTIMATED SITE VALUE | = $ | 250 |
| (If leasehold, show only leasehold value.) | | |
| **INDICATED VALUE BY COST APPROACH** | = $ | 685 |

(Not Required by Freddie Mac and Fannie Mae)

Does property conform to applicable HUD/VA property standards? [X] Yes [ ] No

If No, explain: _____

Construction Warranty [ ] Yes [x] No

Name of Warranty Program _____

Warranty Coverage Expires _____

The undersigned has recited three recent sales of properties most similar and proximate to subject and has considered these in the market analysis. The description includes a dollar adjustment, reflecting market reaction to those items of significant variation between the subject and comparable properties. If a significant item in the comparable property is superior to, or more favorable than, the subject property, a minus (–) adjustment is made, thus reducing the indicated value of subject; if a significant item in the comparable is inferior to, or less favorable than, the subject property, a plus (+) adjustment is made, thus increasing the indicated value of the subject.

**SALES COMPARISON ANALYSIS**

| ITEM | SUBJECT | COMPARABLE NO. 1 | | COMPARABLE NO. 2 | | COMPARABLE NO. 3 | |
|---|---|---|---|---|---|---|---|
| Address | 5700 Granada | 5618 Riviera Dr | | 3441 Alhambra Circle | | 4040 Kiora | |
| Proximity to Subject | | 1 mile south | | 1 mile NW | | 3/8 mile ESE | |
| Sales Price | $ NA | $ 715,000 | | $ 765,000 | | $ 703,000 | |
| Price/Gross Liv. Area | $ ☑ | $ 155.50 ☑ | | $ 144.09 ☑ | | $ 121.82 ☑ | |
| Data Source | REDI, PR | REDI, PR | | REDI, PR | | REDI, PR | |
| VALUE ADJUSTMENTS | DESCRIPTION | DESCRIPTION | + (–)$ Adjustment | DESCRIPTION | + (–)$ Adjustment | DESCRIPTION | + (–)$ Adjustment |
| Sales or Financing Concessions | | Not Avail | (in $000s) | Not Avail | (in $000s) | Not Avail | (in $000s) |
| Date of Sale/Time | Not applicable | 1/89 | 24 | 6/89 | 9 | 4/89 | 15 |
| Location | Coral Gables | Coral Gabels | | Coral Gables | | Miami | 20 |
| Site/View | .5Ac/Canal/Pool | .8Ac/Canal/Pool | –20 | .9Ac/Canal/Pool | –35 | .5Ac/Pool | 25 |
| Design and Appeal | Ran/Av | Ran/Av | | Ran/Av | | Ran/Av | |
| Quality of Construction | Av CBS 1 Sty | Av CBS 1 Sty | | Av CBS 1 Sty | | Av CBS 2 Sty | |
| Age | 1953 | 1950 | | 1955 | | 1949 | |
| Condition | Fair | Av; recently remod. | – 18 | Av; recently remod. | – 18 | Good; recently remod. | – 43 |
| Above Grade | Total Bdrms Baths | Total Bdrms Baths | | Total Bdrms Baths | | Total Bdrms Baths | |
| Room Count | 10 4 4½ | 4 3 | | 5 5 | | 6 8 | |
| Gross Living Area | 5084 Sq. Ft. | 3908 Sq. Ft. | 25 | 4513 Sq. Ft. | | 4905 Sq. Ft. | |
| Basement & Finished Rooms Below Grade | 0 | 0 | | 0 | | 0 | |
| Functional Utility | Av | Av | | Av | | Av | |
| Heating/Cooling | RevCyc Cent A/C | RevCyc Cent A/C | | RevCyc Cent A/C | | RevCyc Cent A/C | |
| Garage/Carport | 4 Car garage | None | 20 | 2 Car Garage | 10 | 2 Car carport | 15 |
| Porches, Patio, Pools, etc. | Wd dock, fen, patio, pool | Wd dock, fen, patio, pool | | Conc dock, fen patio, pool | 10 | Fen, patio, pool | 15 |
| Special Energy Efficient Items | boat storage | boat storage | | | | | |
| Fireplace(s) | 1 | | | 0 | 2 | 1 | |
| Other (e.g. kitchen equip., remodeling) | see CONDITION item above | | | | | | |
| Net Adj. (total) | | [X] + [ ] – $ 31,000 | | [ ] + [ ] – $ 22,000 | | [X] + [ ] – $ 47,000 | |
| Indicated Value of Subject | | $ 746,000 | | $ 743,000 | | $ 750,000 | |

Comments on Sales Comparison: (1) For this price bracket home, overimprovement = 4500+ living sq ft, more than 4 bedrooms or more than 3 baths. Living sf = Adj sf x .85, thus: 5981sf x .86 + 5084 living sf. (subject) This is for comparison with the comparables.

INDICATED VALUE BY SALES COMPARISON APPROACH .................................................. $ 745,000

INDICATED VALUE BY INCOME APPROACH (If Applicable) Estimated Market Rent $ Not applica (1) Mo. x Gross Rent Multiplier _____ = $ _____

This appraisal is made [ ] "as is" [ ] subject to the repairs, alterations, inspections or conditions listed below [ ] completion per plans and specifications.

Comments and Conditions of Appraisal: _____

Final Reconciliation: _____

**RECONCILIATION**

This appraisal is based upon the above requirements, the certification, contingent and limiting conditions, and Market Value definition that are stated in

[ ] FmHA, HUD &/or VA instructions.

[ ] Freddie Mac Form 439 (Rev. 7/86)/Fannie Mae Form 1004B (Rev. 7/86) filed with client _____ 19 _____ [ ] attached.

I (WE) ESTIMATE THE MARKET VALUE, AS DEFINED, OF THE SUBJECT PROPERTY AS OF _____ 19 _____ to be $ _____

I (We) certify: that to the best of my (our) knowledge and belief the facts and data used herein are true and correct; that I (we) personally inspected the subject property, both inside and out, and have made an exterior inspection of all comparable sales cited in this report; and that I (we) have no undisclosed interest, present or prospective therein.

| Appraiser(s) SIGNATURE _____ | Review Appraiser SIGNATURE _____ (if applicable) | [ ] Did [ ] Did Not |
|---|---|---|
| NAME _____ | NAME _____ | Inspect Property |

Freddie Mac Form 70 10/86 (10 ch.)     BLAKEWOOD BUSINESS FORMS 1 (800) 443-1004     Fannie Mae Form 1004 10/86

**Comp #1**

| | |
|---|---|
| BUYER: EDELMANN JULIUS J | SALE DT   01-20-89 |
| MADDR:   5618 RIVIERA DR | REC DT   01-25-89 |
|           CORAL GABLES, FL 33146 | SALES AMT          $715,000 |
| SELLER:   GETZ, RICHARD | MTG AMT          $500,000 |
| MTG NAME: DADELAND BK | STAMP AMT          $3,828.50 |
|           BLK 127 LOT 53 | MTG TYPE: CNV |
| LEGAL - LT 10 LESS N 38 ALL LT 11 12 | DEED TYPE: WD |
|           LESS S48 ALL IN BLK 128 PB | BK/PG 13972-3083 |

31 /1 TOG WITH ALL LANDS LYING BETWEEN W LINE
SHORELINE CORAL GABLES WATERWAY

**Comp #2**

| | |
|---|---|
| FOLIO 03-4118-006-0120 | SALE DT   05-26-89 |
| SITUS:   3441 ALHAMBRA CIR | REC DT   06-01-89 |
|           CORAL GABLES, FL 33134 | SALE AMT:          $765,000 |
| BUYER:   3441 ALHAMBRA CIR | STAMP AMT:          $4,207.50 |
| MADDR:   3441 ALHAMBRA CIR | DEED TYPE: WD |
|           CORAL GABLES, FL 33134 | BK/PG 14129-708 |
| SELLER:   RIESGO ARMANDO | LAND ASSMT:          $269,494 |
|           BLK 50 LOT 19 | IMPR ASSMT:          $201,408 |
|  *LAND USE - 01 SINGLE FAMILY | TAXES (88)          $10,352.47 |
|  *PRIOR SALE - $675,000  5-88 | *C/L FENCE, CENT A/C T |
|  *BATHS - 5 | *DOCK CONCR, FLAG/PATIO |
|  *BDRMS - 5 | *ADJ SQ FT - 5,309 |
|  *YEAR BUILT - 1955 | *POOL W/WHL |

LEGAL - LTS 19 20 21 22 & THAT POR LTS 23 24 25 DECS BEG AT NW COR LT 23 . SELY
ALG C/L CANAL ON E LINE LT 25 WHICH IS 11 NWLY SE COR LT 25, NWLY ALG ELY LINE
LTS 23-25 TO NE COR LT 23, WLY ALG NLY LINE LT 23 TO POB ALL BLK 50 PB 10/57 PCI,
MAY ALSO DESC AS LTS 19 20 21 & THAT POR LTS 22 23 24 25 LYING N WATERWAY &
BEING BET C/L WATERWAY & LT 21 ALL BLK 50

**Comp #3**

| | |
|---|---|
| FOLIO 01-4129-007-0110 | SALE DT   05-02-89 |
| SITUS:   4040 KIAORA ST | REC DT   05-04-89 |
|           MIAMI, FL 33133 | SALE AMT          $702,500 |
| BUYER:   DAVIS, ALVIN B. | MTG AMT          $475,000 |
| MADDR:   4040 KIAORA ST | STAMP AMT          $3,863.75 |
|           MIAMI, FL | MTG TYPE: CNV |
| SELLER: KIRKPATRICK, JR. HOME | DEED TYPE: WD |
| MTG NAME: NORTHERN TRUST BANK FL | BK/PG 14096-686 |
|           TRACT 16 | LAND ASSMT:          $236,805 |
|  *LAND USE - 01 SINGLE FAMILY | IMPR ASSMT:          $199,075 |
|  *PRIOR SALE - $110,000  6-73 | TAXES (88)          $12,213.42 |
|  *BATHS - 6 | *C/L FENCE, CENT A/C T |
|  *BDRMS - 8 | *CON/PATIO, WALL CBS |
|  *YEAR BUILT- 1949 | *WALL ORN/B |
|  *POOL 6' | *ADJ SQ FT - 5,771 |
| LEGAL - LT 166 PB 41/37 | |

**Microfiche Tax Roll (Redi Sales Book)**

03-4129-026-0040 TW 54 RG 41 SC 29 SUB 026 01 - SINGLE FAMILY    14 - SINGLE FAMILY
BLK - 128 LOT - 24  MILL - 30 STATE USE 01      ADJ SQFT - 5,981    PRICE $700,000      $849,000 -TV
                    89-PEBBLE PAT    6-BOAT STG C      PRICE/SQFT $117.04      9/84  R    $458,460 -LV
                    88-TERR/PATIO   20-DOCK WD/CO      BEDROOMS -3                        $388,540 -IV
                    2-CENT A/C T   135-WALL ORN/B      BATHS      -3.0                    $19,415.09 -TX
                    102-POOL 8' AV                     YEAR BUILT -1953    EXEMPT CODES -H
5700 GRANADA BLVD      CORAL GABLES FL 33146
C GABLES RIVIERA SEC 9 PB 28-29 LOTS 24 & 25 & STRIP BETWEEN
LOTS & WATERWAY BLK 128 LOT SIZE IRREGULAR OR 12277-0179 0984          140X150

What is the comparative sales analysis reduction in tax dollars saved?

---

**Case 3. TAX REDUCTION DATA Scratchsheet.**

| | Subject | Comp 1 | Comp 2 | Comp 3 |
|---|---|---|---|---|
| **Address** | _____ | _____ | _____ | _____ |
| **Sales price** | _____[1] | _____ | _____ | _____ |
| **Sq ft[2]** | _____ | _____ | _____ | _____ |
| **$__/sf** | _____ | _____ | _____ | _____ |
| **Lot size** | _____ | _____ | _____ | _____ |
| **Sale date[3]** | _____ | _____ | _____ | _____ |
| **Bd/Ba** | _____ | _____ | _____ | _____ |
| **Dist from subj** | 0 | _____ | _____ | _____ |
| **Yr blt** | 19_____ | 19_____ | 19_____ | 19_____ |

Mean$/sf[4] = $ _____ ÷ 3 × [Subj sf] × 0.9[5] = $ _____ proper value. $ _____
less $ _____ = $ _____ assessment reduction × .0 _____ [mills] = $ _____
tax saving from sales analysis and/or home repairs.

[1] $ _____ is the county assessed value, as well as the sales price.

[2] Either adj or liv sf, but not both.

[3] The comparable sales must have occurred in the 12 months before 1/1/89.

[4] Subject lot is little more than half the size of Comp 2 lot. So get a land price estimate (on their stationery, initialed if possible) from a local builder or realtor.

[5] Comp sales must have occurred in the 12 months before 1/1/89.

[6] Mean = [Comp 1 $/sf + Comp 2 + Comp 3] ÷ 3.

[7] CD is 0.9; equal to 10 percent of the sales price as sales expense.

---

## *Case 4: 2960 Carambola—Condo*

Single Family Home FNMA Form 1004 is only slightly different from Condo FNMA Form 1073. The cost approach is not executed on condos because the common elements and budget complicate matters. However, often this omission is compensated for by identical nearby unit sales. One way you can tell is by the taxes. C-1 and the subject have the same

**NEIGHBORHOOD**

Borrower_____ Census Tract_____ Map Reference_____
Unit No._____ Address 2960 Carambola Circle South ___ Project Name/Phase No._____
City_____ County_____ State_____ Zip Code_____
Actual Real Estate Taxes $_____ (yr.) Sales Price $_____ Property Rights Appraised ☐ Fee ☒ Leasehold
Loan Charges to be Paid by Seller $_____ Other Sales Concessions_____
Lender/Client_____ Lender's Address_____
Occupant_____ Appraiser_____ Instructions to Appraiser_____
☐ FNMA 1073A required    ☐ FHLMC 465 Addendum A required    ☐ FHLMC 465 Addendum B required

| Location | ☐ Urban | ☒ Suburban | ☐ Rural |
|---|---|---|---|
| Built up | ☐ Over 75% | ☒ 25% to 75% | ☐ Under 25% |
| Growth Rate | ☐ Fully Developed | ☒ Rapid (1) | ☐ Steady | ☐ Slow |
| Property Values | | ☒ Increasing | ☐ Stable | ☐ Declining |
| Demand/Supply | | ☐ Shortage | ☒ In Balance | ☐ Oversupply |
| Marketing Time | | ☒ Under 3 Mos. (1) | ☐ 4-6 Mos. | ☐ Over 6 Mos. |

Present Land Use ____ % 1 Family ____ % 2-4 Family ____ % Apts 100 ____ % Condo
____ % Commercial ____ % Industrial ____ % Vacant
Change in Present Land Use ☐ Not Likely ☐ Likely* ☐ Taking Place*
* From ____ To ____

Predominant Occupancy ☐ Owner ☐ Tenant ____ % Vacant
Condominium: Price Range $ 60000 to $ 85000 Predominant $ ____
Age ____ yrs. to ____ yrs. Predominant ____ yrs.
Single Family: Price Range $ ____ to $ ____ Predominant $ ____
Age ____ yrs. to ____ yrs. Predominant ____ yrs.

Describe potential for additional Condo/PUD units in nearby area Vacant land N of
Sample Rd: Lot Line SFH or Condo. (1) Pre-const sales; Bldr sellout ahead of sched. (2) Police Stat.

NEIGHBORHOOD RATING

| | Good | Avg. | Fair | Poor |
|---|---|---|---|---|
| Adequacy of Shopping | ☐ | ☒ | ☐ | ☐ |
| Employment Opportunities | ☐ | ☒ | ☐ | ☐ |
| Recreational Facilities | ☐ | ☒ | ☐ | ☐ |
| Adequacy of Utilities | ☐ | ☒ | ☐ | ☐ |
| Property Compatibility | ☐ | ☒ | ☐ | ☐ |
| Protection from Detrimental Conditions | ☐ | ☒ | ☐ | ☐ |
| Police and Fire Protection | ☒ (2) | ☒ | ☐ | ☐ |
| General Appearance of Properties | ☐ | ☒ | ☐ | ☐ |
| Appeal to Market | ☐ | ☒ | ☐ | ☐ |

| | Distance | Access or Convenience |
|---|---|---|
| Public Transportation | 1 mi | ☒ |
| Employment Centers | 3 mi | ☒ |
| Neighborhood Shopping | 2 mi | ☒ |
| Grammar Schools | 2 mi | ☒ |
| Freeway Access | 2 mi | ☒ |

NOTE: FHLMC/FNMA do not consider race or the racial composition of the neighborhood to be reliable appraisal factors.

Describe those factors, favorable or unfavorable, affecting marketability (e.g. public parks, schools, noise, view, mkt. area, population size and financial ability).
Tradewinds Park and Bird Sanctuary abuts S side of subj project. Earth covered "Mt Trashmore" apx 200' high, 200 yds
600 yds long, .5 miles N of Subj does not seems to adversely affect value

**SITE**

Lot Dimensions (if PUD) Multi family ____ = ____ Sq. Ft. ☐ Corner Lot Project Density When Completed as Planned 4.5 Units/Acre
Zoning Classification _____ Present improvements ☒ do ☐ do not conform to zoning regulations
Highest and best use: ☒ Present use ☐ Other (specify) (1) 5400 units on 1200 acres

| | Public | Other (Describe) | OFF-SITE IMPROVEMENTS | | |
|---|---|---|---|---|---|
| Elec. | ☒ | | Street Access: ☒ Public ☐ Private | | |
| Gas | ☐ | | Surface Asphalt | | |
| Water | ☒ | | Maintenance: ☒ Public ☐ Private | | |
| San. Sewer | ☒ | | ☒ Storm Sewer ☐ Curb/Gutter | | |
| ☒ Underground Elec. & Tel. | | | ☒ Sidewalk ☒ Street Lights | | |

Project Ingress/Egress (adequacy) Good
Topo Level, with lakes throughout property
Size/Shape Irregular; see maps
View Amenity Residential/Lake
Drainage/Flood Conditions Appears adequate
Is the property located in a HUD identified Special Flood Hazard Area? ☐ No ☒ Yes

(1) 5400 units on 1200 acres ... encroachments or other adverse conditions) Zone A1 El 14' FEMA Map 120031 0005 C. Aplwd IV is a
premium (Adults Only – subj to Fl A.O. litigation) one of 38 assns comprising. Aplwd Master Condo Assn

**PROJECT IMPROVEMENTS**

| TYPE | ☒ Existing |
|---|---|
| | ☒ Condo ☐ PUD |
| | ☐ Proposed |

Approx. Year Built 19 88 Original Use Condo
☐ Converted (19___)
☐ Under Construction
PROJECT ☐ Under Construction
☒ Elevator (Subj Bldg) ☐ Walk-up No. of Stories 1 in subject bldg
☐ Row or Town House ☐ Other (specify)
☒ Primary Residence ☐ Second Home or Recreational

If Completed: No. Phases 38 No. Units 5400 No. Sold 5398
If Incomplete: Planned No. Phases 38 No. Units 5400 No. Sold 5398
Units in Subject Phase: Total ____ Completed ____ Sold ____ Rented ____
Approx. No. Units for Sale: Total Project 2 Subject Phase 2

PROJECT RATING

| | Good | Avg. | Fair | Poor |
|---|---|---|---|---|
| Location | ☐ | ☒ | ☐ | ☐ |
| General Appearance | ☐ | ☒ | ☐ | ☐ |
| Amenities and Recreational Facilities | ☐ | ☒ | ☐ | ☐ |
| Density (units per acre) | ☐ | ☒ | ☐ | ☐ |
| Unit Mix | ☐ | ☒ | ☐ | ☐ |
| Quality of Constr. (mat'l & finish) | ☐ | ☒ | ☐ | ☐ |
| Condition of Exterior New | ☒ | ☒ | ☐ | ☐ |
| Condition of Interior New, clean | ☒ | ☒ | ☐ | ☐ |
| Appeal to Market Good | ☒ | ☒ | ☐ | ☐ |

Exterior Wall CBS Roof Covering T&G Security Features None
Elevator: No. 0 Adequacy & Condition NA Soundproofing: Vertical Adequate Horizontal Adequate 104
Parking: Total No. Spaces 270 Ratio 1.0 + Guest Spaces/Unit Type Assigned No. Spaces of Guest Parking ____
Describe common elements or recreational facilities Aplwd IV Asn: Pool, Rec room, lake. Master Asn: See SUBJECT UNIT comments
Are any common facilities, rec. facilities or parking leased to Owners Assoc.? ____ If yes, attach addendum describing rental, terms and options.

**SUBJECT UNIT**

☒ Existing ☐ Proposed ☐ Under Constr. Floor No. 2 Unit Livable Area 1222 ☐ Basement 0 % Finished ____
Parking for Unit: No. 1 Type Off st ☒ Assigned ☐ Owned Convenience to Unit Steps away

| Room List | Foyer | Liv | Din | Kit | Bdrm | Bath | Fam | Rec | Lndry | Other |
|---|---|---|---|---|---|---|---|---|---|---|
| Basement | | | | | | | | | | |
| 1st Level | | | | | | | | | | |
| 2nd Level | Area | Area | Area | 1 | 3 | 2 | | | Area | Porch |

UNIT RATING

| | Good | Avg. | Fair | Poor |
|---|---|---|---|---|
| Condition of Improvement | ☒ | ☐ | ☐ | ☐ |
| Room Sizes and Layout | ☐ | ☒ | ☐ | ☐ |
| Adequacy of Closets and Storage | ☐ | ☒ | ☐ | ☐ |
| Kit. Equip., Cabinets & Workspace | ☐ | ☒ | ☐ | ☐ |
| Plumbing—Adequacy and Condition | ☐ | ☒ | ☐ | ☐ |
| Electrical—Adequacy and Condition | ☐ | ☒ | ☐ | ☐ |
| Adequacy of Soundproofing | ☐ | ☒ | ☐ | ☐ |
| Adequacy of Insulation | ☐ | ☒ | ☐ | ☐ |
| Location within Project or View | ☐ | ☒ | ☐ | ☐ |
| Overall Livability | ☒ | ☒ | ☐ | ☐ |
| Appeal and Marketability | ☒ | ☒ | ☐ | ☐ |

| Floors: | ☐ Hardwood | ☒ Carpet over cement | ☒ Kit, Ba tile |
|---|---|---|---|
| Int. Walls: | ☒ Drywall | ☐ Plaster | |
| Trim/Finish: | ☐ Good | ☒ Average | ☐ Fair ☐ Poor |
| Bath Floor: | ☒ Ceramic | ☐ Wainscot ☒ Ceramic | |

Windows (type): Sing Hung ____ ☐ Storm Sash ☒ Screens ☐ Combo
Kitchen Equip: ☒ Refrig. ☒ Range/Oven ☒ Fan/Hood ☒ Washer ☒ Dryer
☐ Intercom ☐ Disposal ☒ Dishwasher ☒ Microwave ☐ Compactor

HEAT: Type Rev Cycle Fuel Elec Cond Good
AIR COND: ☒ Central ☐ Other ☐ Adequate ☐ Inadequate

Est. Effective Age 0 to 1 yrs.
Est. Remaining Economic Life 54 to 55 yrs.

☐ Earth Sheltered Housing Design ☐ Solar Design/Landscape ☐ Solar Space Heat/Air Cond. ☐ Solar Hot Water
☐ Flue Damper ☐ Elec./Mech. Gas Furn. Ignition ☐ Auto Setback Thermostat ☒ Dble./Triple Glazed Windows ☐ Caulk/Weatherstrip
INSULATION (state R-Factor if known) ☒ Walls R 10 ☐ Ceiling ☐ Floor ☒ Roof/Attic R19 ☒ Water Heater ____

If rehab proposed, do plans and specs provide for adequate energy conservation? ____ If no, attach description of modification needed.
ENERGY EFFICIENCY APPEARS: ☐ High ☒ Adequate ☐ Low Energy Audit: ☐ Yes (attach, if available) ☒ No

COMMENTS (special features, functional or physical inadequacies, modernization or repairs needed, etc.) Master Condo Assn, Olym pool, Conf Cntr,
Performance Ctr (U/C), lobby, sports ctr, billards, cards and other rooms. No physical inadequacies noted by appraiser
during 2/14/89 inspection.

Unit Charge $ 333 + 63/Qtr /Mo. x 12 = $ _____ /Yr. ($ 97 /Sq. Ft./year of livable area) Ground Rent (if any) $ 0 /yr.

Utilities included in unit charge: ☐ None ☐ Heat ☐ Air Cond. ☐ Electricity ☐ Gas ☒ Water ☒ Sewer

Note any fees, other than regular Condo/PUD charges, for use of facilities: None. (1) Aplwd IV $333/Qtr + Aplwd Master Asn $63/qtr

To properly maintain the project and provide the services anticipated, the budget appears: ☐ High ☒ Adequate ☐ Inadequate

Compared to other competitive projects of similar quality and design subject unit charge appears: ☐ High ☒ Reasonable ☐ Low

Management Group: ☐ Owners Association ☐ Developer ☐ Management Agent (identify) Summit Mgt Co

Quality of Management and it's enforcement of Rules and Regulations appears: ☐ Superior ☒ Good ☐ Adequate ☐ Inadequate

Special or unusual characteristics in the Condo/PUD Documents or otherwise known to the appraiser, that would affect marketability (if none, so state) (1) Budget will rise as units age. (2) Summit Mgt assumed control from Twp Mgt Serv Inc on 2/9/89

Comments: Aolwd IV Budget attached; Master Assn budget will be forwarded when available.

NOTE: FHLMC does not require the cost approach in the appraisal of condominium or PUD units.

Cost Approach (to be used only for detached, semi-detached, and town house units):

Reproduction Cost New ____ Sq. Ft. @ $ ____ per Sq. Ft. = ................ $ NA

Less Depreciation: Physical $ ____ Functional $ ____ Economic $ ____ ( ____ )

Depreciated Value of Improvements: ........................... ____

Add Land Value (if leasehold, show only leasehold value—attach calculations) ........... ____

Pro-rata Share of Value of Amenities ........................... ____

Total Indicated Value: ☐ FEE SIMPLE ☐ LEASEHOLD ........................ $ ____

Comments regarding estimate of depreciation and value of land and amenity package ____

The appraiser, whenever possible, should analyze two comparable sales from within the subject project. However, when appraising a unit in a new or newly converted project, at least two comparables should be selected from outside the subject project. In the following analysis, the comparable should always be adjusted to the subject unit and not vice versa. If a significant feature of the comparable is superior to the subject unit, a minus (—) adjustment should be made to the comparable; if such a feature of the comparable is inferior to the subject, a plus (+) adjustment should be made to the comparable.

**LIST ONLY THOSE ITEMS THAT REQUIRE ADJUSTMENT**

| ITEM | Subject Property | COMPARABLE NO. 1 | +(—)$ Adjustment | COMPARABLE NO. 2 | +(—)$ Adjustment | COMPARABLE NO. 3 | +(—)$ Adjustment |
|---|---|---|---|---|---|---|---|
| Address-Unit No: Project Name | 2960 Carambola Circle S | 2962 Carambola Circle So. | | 2651 Carambola Circle N | | 2633 Carambola Circle N | |
| Proximity to Subj. | | | | | | | |
| Sales Price | $ 80,900 | $ 80,900 | | $ 78,000 | | $ 80,000 | |
| Price/Living Area | $ 66.20 | $ 66.20 | | $ 63.83 | | $ 64.00 | |
| Data Source | REDI, inspection | REDI | | REDI | | REDI | |
| Date of Sale and Time Adjustment | DESCRIPTION 9/88 | DESCRIPTION 9/88 | | DESCRIPTION 9/88 | | DESCRIPTION 12/88 | |
| Location | 2 Fl, SE Cor | 2 Fl, SW Cor (1) | | 1 Fl, NE Cor (1) | | 1 Fl, NE Cor (1) | |
| Site/View | Lake/Res | Lake/Res | | Lake/Res | | Lake/Res | |
| Design and Appeal | 2Sty8 Plex/Av | 2Sty8plex/Av | | 2Sty8Plex/Av | | 1Sty4Plex/Av(2) | -1000 |
| Quality of Constr. | CBS Av | CBS Av | | CBS Av | | CBS Av | |
| Age | 1988 | 1988 | | 1984 | | 1984 | 3000 |
| Condition | Good | Good | | Good | | Good | |
| Living Area, Room Count & Total | Total 5 : B-rms 3 : Baths 2 | Total 5 : B-rms 3 : Baths 2 | | Total 5 : B-rms 3 : Baths 2 | | Total 4 : B-rms 2 : Baths 2 | 1000 |
| Gross Living Area | 1222 Sq. Ft. | 1222 Sq. Ft. | | 1222 Sq. Ft. | | 1250 Sq. Ft. | |
| Basement & Bsmt. | 0 | 0 | | 0 | | 0 | |
| Finished Rooms | | | | | | | |
| Functional Utility | Av | Av | | Av | | Av | |
| Air Conditioning | Cent | Cent | | Cent | | Cent | |
| Storage | 60 cu ft | 60 cu ft | | 60 cu ft | | 60 cu ft | |
| Parking Facilities | 1 + guest | 1 + guest | | 1 + guest | | 1 + guest | |
| Common Elements and Recreation Facilities | Pool, rec bldg, Lake + Olym Pool Hall etc (Master Assn) | Same. See Page 1 | | Same | | Same | |
| Mo. Assessment | $396/Qtr tot (3) | $396/Qtr tot (3) | | $393 Qtr tot (3) | | $396 Qtr tot (3) | |
| Leasehold/Fee | None | None | | None | | None | |
| Special Energy Efficient Items | No | No | | No | | No | |
| Other (e.g. fire-places, kitchen equip., remodeling) | Flat T&G roof Por | Flat T&G roof Por | | Flat T&G roof Por | | Pitched tile roof Por | - 2000 |
| Sales or Financing Concessions | Bldr sale | Bldr sale | | Private sale | | Private sale | |
| Net Adj. (total) | | ☐ Plus ☐ Minus $ | 0 | ☒ Plus ☐ Minus $ | 3000 | ☒ Plus ☐ Minus $ | 1000 |
| Indicated value of Subject | | $ | 80,900 | $ | 81,000 | $ | 81,000 |

Comments on Market Data Analysis (1) 2Fl - security vs 1Fl convenience & lake view vs pvt garden; washes. (2) More privacy & quiet. Comps equally weighted. (3) Applewood IV $$333 + master Asn $63 = $396/Qtr)

INDICATED VALUE BY MARKET DATA APPROACH ........................... $ 81,000

INDICATED VALUE BY INCOME APPROACH (if applicable) Economic Market Rent $ 950 /Mo. x Gross Rent Multiplier 86 = $ 81,000

This appraisal is made ☒ "as is" ☐ subject to repairs, alterations, or conditions listed below ☐ subject to completion per plans and specifications.

Comments and Conditions of Appraisal: $63/Qtrx5400 units = $1,360,000 ann budget for master assn. This budget will be forwarded when available (under separate cover) from Summit Prop Mgt Co (305) 792 6000. On 2/17/89 budget data was still in Bldr (Twp Mgt Serv Co) hands.

Final Reconciliation: Market data analysis is primary criterion of value, due to rental paucity. Value: $81,000. Information sources: Minto Corp Office: (305) 973 4490; Ap IV Asn Pres MaxBond 978-6907, Summit Prop Mgt Co (above)

Construction Warranty ☒ Yes ☐ No Name of Warranty Program _____ Warranty Coverage Expires 1-8 yrs depending on item certific.

This appraisal is based upon the above requirements, the certification, contingent and limiting conditions, and Market Value definition that are stated in ☐ & addendum

☐ FHLMC Form 439 (Rev. 10/78)/FNMA Form 1004B (Rev. 10/78) filed with client ____ 19 ____

I ESTIMATE THE MARKET VALUE, AS DEFINED, OF SUBJECT PROPERTY AS OF ____ 19 ____ to be $ 81,000

Appraiser(s) Henry W. Willen for Willen Associates Inc. Review Appraiser (if applicable) ____

Date Report Signed ____ 19 ____ ☐ Did ☐ Did Not Physically Inspect Property

FHLMC Form 465 9/10 REVERSE Forms and Worms, Incorporated, 315 Whitney Ave., New Haven CT 06511 1-800-243-4545 LLLP FNMA Form 1073 9/80

**Subject**
FOLIO 48-42-20-00-0000
BUYER:
MADDR:

SELLER:   MINTO BUILDERS INC
MTG NAME: HOMESTEAD FEDERAL SAVINGS
           UNIT 2040
LEGAL - PCL 2040 BLDG 5 OR 15681/642

| | |
|---|---|
| SALE DT   09-20-88 | |
| REC DT   09-23-88 | |
| SALES AMT | $80,900 |
| MTG AMT | $64,700 |
| STAMP AMT: | $444.95 |
| MTG TYPE: CNV | |
| DEED TYPE:  WD | |
| BK/PG 15807-95 | |

**Comp #1**
FOLIO 48-42-20-00-0000
BUYER:   KING, RAYNOLD A.
MADDR:   2963 S. CARAMBOLA CIR
           COCONUT CREEK, FL
SELLER:   MINOT BUILDERS INC
MTG NAME: COMMONWEALTH SAVINGS
           UNIT 2037
LEGAL - PCL 2037 BLDG 5 OR 15681/642

| | |
|---|---|
| SALE DT   09-16-88 | |
| REC DT   09-20-88 | |
| SALE AMT | $80,900 |
| MTG AMT | $64,700 |
| STAMP AMT | $444.95 |
| MTG TYPE: CNV | |
| DEED TYPE: WD | |
| BK/PG 15796-132 | |

**Comp #2**
BUYER:   IMPERATO, JOHN A.
MADDR:   2651 N. CARAMBOLA CIR
           COCONUT CREEK  FL 33066
SELLER:   ZIMMERMAN, ELLIOT M
           UNIT 1753
LEGAL - PCL 1737 BLDG 8 OR 13373/427

| | |
|---|---|
| SALE DT   09-08-88 | |
| REC DT   09-13-88 | |
| SALE AMT | $78,000 |
| STAMP AMT | $429.00 |
| DEED TYPE: WD | |
| BK/PG 15778-777 | |

**Comp #3**
FOLIO 48-42-20-CM-019
BUYER:   HOLLAND, JEROME
MADDR:   2632 N. CARAMBOLA CIR
SELLER:   JOHNSON, HAROLD S.
MTG NAME: HOME SAVINGS  UNIT 1719
  *LAND USE - 04 CONDOMINIUM
  *PRIOR SALE - $71,900  10-86W
LEGAL - UNIT  1719 BLDG 5 OR 13373/427

| | |
|---|---|
| SALE DT   11-30-88 | |
| REC DT   12-05-88 | |
| SALE AMT | $80,000 |
| MTG AMT | $60,000 |
| MTG TYPE: CNV | |
| DEED TYPE: WD | |
| LAND ASSMT | $5,900 |
| IMPR ASSMT | $53,130 |
| TOTAL ASSMT | $59,030 |
| TAXES (87) | $1,141.83 |

**APPLEWOOD VILLAGE**

($444.95) stamp amount. A site inspection revealed identical units (same window and door layout, outside measurements, and so forth). Note that the unit square footage, year built, and so forth are not given in the Sales Data. The appraiser found this information by checking the tax roll, or by talking to the Condo Association, getting floor plans.

Given: The condo association has provided unit owners with a receipt for a $5,000 prorated extraordinary roof repair in 1988. Condo appraisers must use the FNMA Condo Form 1073, not the Single Family 1004. Look at Exhibit G2's items of comparison on the comparable sales analysis section of 1073's page 2. For our purposes, the main differences are the following items: (1) **monthly condo assessment** (for common elements' maintenance); (2) **common elements** (pool, rec room, tennis courts, and so forth); (3) **parking** (how many and what type spaces). These items are unique to condos and coops, for the most part. Get what information you can from the REDI sheet, and the rest from the FNMA Form 1073 Sales Comparison Analysis appraisal. Use 26 mills as the county millage.

A. What is the Comparative Sales Analysis reduction in tax dollars saved?

B. How many tax dollars are saved via the roof repair?

C. What is subject (1) monthly assessment; (2) common elements; (3) parking spaces?

Note Condo Form 1073 (not 1004) Sales Comparison Analysis Item "MONTHLY ASSESSMENT" (maintenance, and so forth), and other items unique to condos, such as number of parking spaces, common elements.

---

**Case 4.  TAX REDUCTION DATA Scratchsheet.**

|                        | Subject        | Comp 1          | Comp 2          | Comp 3          |
|------------------------|----------------|-----------------|-----------------|-----------------|
| **Address**            | _____  | _____   | _____   | _____   |
| **Sales price**        | _____[1]   | _____   | _____   | _____   |
| **Sq ft[2]**           | _____  | _____   | _____   | _____   |
| **$__/sf**             | _____  | _____   | _____   | _____   |
| **Lot size**           | _____  | _____   | _____   | _____   |
| **Sale date[3]**       | _____  | _____   | _____   | _____   |
| **Bd/Ba**              | _____  |                 |                 |                 |
| **Dist from subj**     | 0              | _____   | _____   | _____   |
| **Yr blt**             | 19_____    | 19_____     | 19_____     | 19_____     |
| **Mo assessment**      | $_____   | _____   | _____   | _____   |
| **Common elements**    | _____  | _____   | _____   | _____   |
| **Parking**            | _____  | _____   | _____   | _____   |

Mean$/sf[4] = \$    ÷ 3 ×    [Subj sf] × $0.9^5$ = \$    proper value. \$
less \$    = \$    assessment reduction × .0    [mills] = \$
tax saving from sales analysis and/or home repairs.

[1] \$    is the county assessed value, not the sales price.
[2] Either adj or liv sf, but not both.
[3] The comparable sales must have occurred in the 12 months before 1/1/89.
[4] Mean = [Comp 1 \$/sf + Comp 2 + Comp 3] ÷ 3.
[5] In this case, the CD is 100 percent of the market value.

---

## Case 4.  TAX REDUCTION DATA.

|  | Subject | Comp 1 | Comp 2 | Comp 3 |
|---|---|---|---|---|
| **Address** | 2960 Carambola | 2962 Carambola | 2651 Carambola | 2633 Carambola |
| **Sales price** | $80,900[1] | $80,900 | $78,000 | $80,000 |
| **Sq ft[2]** | 1,222 | 1,222 | 1,222 | 1,250 |
| **$__/sf** | $66.20/sf | $66.20/sf | $63.83/sf | $64.00/sf |
| **Lot size[3]** | NA | NA | NA | NA |
| **Sale date[4]** | 9/88 | 9/88 | 9/88 | 12/88 |
| **Bd/Ba** | 3/2 | 3/2 | 3/2 | 2/2 |
| **Dist from subj** | 0 | Abuts subj W wall | ¼ mi E | ½ mi E |
| **Yr blt** | 1988 | 1988 | 1984 | 1984 |
| **Mo. assessment** | $396/Qtr | $396/Qtr | $393/Qtr | $396/Qtr |
| **Common elements** | Pool, RecBldg, Hall, Olym Pool Lake | Same | Same | Same |
| **Parking** | 1 + Guest | 1 + Guest | 1 + Guest | 1 + Guest |

Mean $/sf[5] = $ _____ × _____ [Subj sf] × $1.0$[6] = $ _____ proper value.
$ _____ less $ _____ = $ _____ assessment reduction × .0260000 (mills) = $ _____
tax saving from sales analysis.

[1] Subject sold in 1988 for $80,900; the price is in line with similar comps; the CD is 100 percent, so assessed and market values are the same; a reduction is improbable.

[2] Either adj or liv sf, but not both.

[3] Condo land is owned by the condo association. The property tax assessment includes a prorated share of the land value in determining the condo "improved value."

[4] Comp sales must have occurred in the 12 months before 1/1/89.

[5] Mean = [Comp 1 $/sf + Comp 2 + Comp 3] ÷ 3.

[6] You cannot deduct 10 percent of the sales price as sales expense because the CD is 1.0.

The prorated $5,000 condo extraordinary roof repairs expense at 26 mills equals **130 tax dollars saved; $5,000 × $.026 = $130.**

## Case 5: 18638 NW 78 Ct.—Single-Family Home

Look at the "recently sold" PRC computer program printouts. Subject is marked S; C1, C2, C3 are the comps. Find the sales date, sold price, Bd/Ba, adj sf, and so forth. Use Indian Creek millage from Exhibit A to determine the tax saving. We have omitted the appraisal form, as it is an unnecessary crutch now. For our purposes, $98,500 is the tax assessed value, not the sales price. The CD is 0.9, or 90 percent of the market value. What is the comparative sales analysis tax saving in dollars?

---

**Case 5.  TAX REDUCTION DATA Scratchsheet.**

|  | Subject | Comp 1 | Comp 2 | Comp 3 |
|---|---|---|---|---|
| **Address** | _____ | _____ | _____ | _____ |
| **Sales price** | _____ [1] | _____ | _____ | _____ |
| **Sq ft** [2] | _____ | _____ | _____ | _____ |
| **$__/sf** | _____ | _____ | _____ | _____ |
| **Lot size** | _____ | _____ | _____ | _____ |
| **Sale date** [3] | _____ | _____ | _____ | _____ |
| **Bd/Ba** | _____ | _____ | _____ | _____ |
| **Dist from subj** | 0 | _____ | _____ | _____ |
| **Yr blt** | 19_____ | 19_____ | 19_____ | 19_____ |

Mean\$/sf [4] = \$      ÷3 ×      [Subj sf] × $0.9$ [5] = \$      proper value. \$      less \$      = \$      assessment reduction × .0      [mills] = \$      tax saving from sales analysis and/or home repairs.

[1] \$      is the county assessed value, not the sales price.
[2] Either adj or liv sf, but not both.
[3] The comparable sales must have occurred in the 12 months before 1/1/89.
[4] Mean = [Comp 1 \$/sf + Comp 2 + Comp 3] ÷ 3.
[5] You can deduct 10 percent of the sales price as sales expense.

## Subject

C-21 FLAGAMI REALTY INC.     262-7444
#M0398513 FLAG    18638 NW 78 CT
MC: 30 20 3 11 0130 SN COUNTRY LAKE    ES:    JH:    TAX ASSESSED VALUE: $98,500    SH:    SALE S /RES
UN:    PB: 129    PG:79    LE: COUNTRY LAKE PARK    DN: ESPLANADE
LR: 18 X14    DR:12 X 12    FR:    KT: 10 X 10    MN: LK TAHOE    SF: 1.280
1 B 14 X12   2B: 12 X 12   3B: 12 X 12    ZN: 37    LS: IRR    YR: 1987    FL:
LP: $98,500
1M: $85,000      1P: 873   PITI    1I: 10.44%    1H: UNIVERSAL
2M: $.00      2P: 0    2I: 0%    2H: 0
MF: 0    RF: 0    TX: $1,200    TY:1987    EQ: $13,500
ON: MUNOZ    LA: MILANES   AP: 558-8989    PH: 2    BC: 2
   L2:    CP:    SC:3
PD: 13/JA/89
SB: FIAG    S2:PETRA    DATE CLOSED 31/JL/88    DP:$13,500

| | | | | |
|---|---|---|---|---|
| SINGLE FAMILY | ONE STORY | 3 BEDROOMS | 2 BATHS | LIVING/DINING |
| COOL - 1 CNT UNIT | OTHER HEATING | RANGE GAS | DISHWASHER | DISPOSER |
| WASHER | WSH/DRY HOOK UP | BURGLAR ALARM | SMOKE DETECTOR | AWNING WINDOWS |
| SHNGL-FIBGL/ASP | CONC BLCK/STCCO | 2 CAR GARAGE | GARAGE-LAUNDRY | SLAB/STRIP PARK |
| NO POOL | SKYLIGHTS | LS: 75 X 100 | LOC-CORNER | NOT WATERFRONT |
| MUNICIPAL WATER ASSOC CONTROL | | 1ST FREE ASSUM | ASSUMPTION-AVL | POSS-CLOSING |
| CALL LO-SHOWING | RESTRC-EXT ALT | ER-EX RGHT SALE | | |
| T | COMPLETE | 17/OC/89   1:25PM | | |

INFORMATION DEEMED RELIABLE BUT NOT GUARANTEED

## Comp #1

ERA AMERICAN DREAM RLTY., #1    621-0131
#M0402918    ERAA1    5871 NW 193 ST    SALE PRICE: $95,000    SALE S /RES
MC: 30 20 1   7 2070 SN: COUNTRY LAKE MANOR    ES: PALMS   JH: L STEV    SH:AMERIC
UN:    PB: 119    PG: 50    LE: LOT 43 BLK 25 OR 12687-136    DN:
LR: 19 X12    DR: 10 X9    FR:    KT: 10 X 9    MN:    SF: 1,401
1B: 14 X 13    2B: 13 X 10    3B: 10 X 10    ZN: 1    LS: 85 X 100    YR: 1985    FL: 1
LP: $99,500
1M: $78,661      1P: 867   PITI    1I: 11.0%    1H: AMERIFIRST
2M: $.00      2P: 0    2I: 0%    2H: 0
MF: 0    RF: 0    TX: $1,395.46    TY: 1987    EQ: $20,839
ON: BORGONIA    LA: KOUTSOFIOS   AP: 989-0945    PH: 2    BC: 2
   L2:    CP:    SC: 3.75
PD: 1/DE/88
SB: ERAA1    S2:0    DC: 16/DC/88    DP: $16,000
SA: KOUTSOFIOS    TS: ASUM    DM: 49

| | | | | |
|---|---|---|---|---|
| SINGLE FAMILY | ONE STORY | 3 BEDROOMS | 2 BATHS | L SHAPED DINING |
| EAT-IN KITCHEN | PANTRY | COOL - 1 CNT UNIT | HEAT - CENT ELEC | RANGE - ELECTRIC |
| REFRIGERATOR | DISHWASHER | WASHER | DRYER | DRAPES & RODS |
| AWNING WINDOWS | SHNGL - FIDGL/ASP | WALL/WALL CRPT | FLR-ASP/RB/VNL | FLR-CUBN/CERAMC |
| CONC BLCK/STCCO | 1 CAR GARAGE | NO POOL | LESS 1/4 ACRE | LOC-CORNER |
| LOC-INTERIOR | NOT WATERFRONT | MUNICIPAL WATER | W-HT ELECTRIC | 1ST-FIXED RATE |
| 1ST-FREE ASSUM | INFO-CALL LO | AVAIL-FHA | AVAIL-VA | AVAL-CONV REFIN. |
| POSS-FUNDING | CALL LO-SHOWING | UNFURNISHED | W/O HOMEST EXMP | ER-EX RGHT SALE |

INFORMATION DEEMED RELIABLE BUT NOT GUARANTEED

## Comp #2

CUPIT REALTY INC.    823-8660
#M0405647 CUPT    6040 NW 201 ST    $95,000    SALE S /RES
MC: 30 20 1   3   4970 SN:COUNTRY LAKE MANOR    ES:CALL    JH:SCHOOL    SH: BOARD
UN:    PB: 117    PG: 74    LE: LOT 2 BLK 15    DN: COUNTRY VILLAGE
LR:    DR:    FR:    KT:    MN:    SF: 1,401
1B:    2B:    3B:    ZN: 1    LS: 78 X 100    YEAR : 1986    FL:
LP: $98,500
1M: $76,937      1P: 768   PITI    1I: 9.5%    1H: UNIVERSAL
2M: $.OO      2P: 0    2I:0%    2H: 00
MF:    RF:    TX $894.48    TY: 1987    EQ: $21,563
ON: QQWITHHELD    LA: LINDA RODDEN   AP: 823-8660    PH: 2    BC: 1
   L2: RESIDENCE    CP: 362-5862    SC: 3.5
PD: 3/JA/89
SB: ASOC2    S2:00    DC: 3/FE/88    DP: $.00
SA: BEDRM    TS: ASUM    DM: 46

| | | | | |
|---|---|---|---|---|
| SINGLE FAMILY | ONE STORY | RANCH | NORTH/SOUTH EXP | 3 BEDROOMS |
| 2 BATHS | LIVING/DINING | L SHAPED DINING | EAT-IN KITCHEN | FLORIDA/ FAM RM |
| ATTIC | COOL - 1CNT UNIT | HEAT - CENT ELEC | RANGE - ELECTRIC | REFRIGERATOR |
| DISHWASHER | DISPOSER | WSH/DRY HOOK-UP | DRAPES & RODS | BLINDS/SHADES |
| REPLACE CHANDLR | AWNING WINDOWS | SLIDE GLASS DR | WALL/WALL CRPT | FLR-ASP/RB/VNL |
| CONC BLCK/STCCO | 1 CAR GARAGE | GARAGE - LAUNDRY | SLAB/STRIP PARK | NO POOL |
| EXTER LIGHTING | LESS 1/4 ACRE | LOC - INTERIOR | NOT WATERPROOF | MUNICIPAL WATER |
| CABLE TV AVAIL | W-HT ELECTRIC | 1ST-FIXED RATE | 1ST-FREE ASSUM | ASSUMPTION-AVL |
| AVAL-CONV REFIN | POSS-FUNDING | CALL LO-SHOWING | FURNISHED | HOMESTEAD EXMPT |
| ER-EX RGHT SALE | | | | |

INFORMATION DEEMED RELIABLE BUT NOT GUARANTEED

## Comp #3

CUPIT REALTY INC.    823-8660
#M0420658    CUPT    8120 NW 191 ST    $93,000    SALE S /RES
MC: 30 20 3   3   0380    SN: LKS OF AVALON    ES:    JH:    SH:
UN:    PB: 125    PG: 44    LE: LOT 12 BLK 3    DN: LKS OF AVALON
LR:    DR:    FR:    KT:    MN:    SF: 1,413
1B:    2B:    3B:    ZN: 0    LS: UNAVAILABLE    YR: 1987    FL:
LP: $101,900
1M: $00      1P:0    00    1I: 0%    1H: 00
2M: $.00      2P: 0    2I: 0%    2H: 00
MF:    RF:    TX: $1,387.62    TY: 1988    EQ: $101,900
ON: QQWITHHELD    LA: DOUG WILSON   AP: 364-2992    PH: 2    BC: 1
   L2:    CP:    SC: 3.%
PD: 1/MY/89
SB: CUPT    S2:0    DC: 30/JN/88    DP: $00
SA: DOUG    TS: CUP    DM: 3

| | | | | |
|---|---|---|---|---|
| SINGLE FAMILY | ONE STORY | 3 BEDROOMS | 2 BATHS | LIVING/DINING |
| COOL - 1 CNT UNIT | COOL - CEIL FAN | HEAT - CENT ELEC | RANGE - ELECTRIC | DISHWASHER |
| DISPOSER | WSH/RY HOOK-UP | BURGLAR ALARM | DRAPES & RODS | VAULTED CEILING |
| FOYER ENTRANCE | SNGL -MTL WINDOW | SHNGL FIBGL/ASP | FLR-ASP/RB/VNL | FLR-CUBN/CERAMC |
| CONC BLCK/STCCO | 1 CAR GARAGE | NO POOL | SKYLIGHTS | LESS 1/4 ACRE |
| LAKE WATERFRONT | MUNICIPAL WATER | SEWER | CABLE TV AVAIL | UNDERGROUND UTI |

## Case 5.　TAX REDUCTION DATA.

|  | Subject | Comp 1 | Comp 2 | Comp 3 |
|---|---|---|---|---|
| **Address** | 18638 NW 78 Ct. | 5871 NW 193 | 6040 NW 201 | 8120 NW 191 |
| **Sales price** | $98,500[1] | $95,000 | $95,000 | $93,000 |
| **Sq ft**[2] | 1,280 adj sf | 1401 adj sf | 1,401 adj sf | 1,410 adj sf |
| **$__/sf** | $76.95/sf | $67.81/sf | $67.81/sf | $65.86/sf |
| **Lot size** | < ¼Ac | < ¼Ac | < ¼Ac | < ¼Ac |
| **Sale date**[3] | NA | 12/88 | 2/88 | 6/88 |
| **Bd/Ba** | 3/2 | 3/2 | 3/2 | 3/2 |
| **Dist from subj** | 0 | 1.5 mi ENE | 1.5 mi ENE | .8 mi W |
| **Yr blt** | 1987 | 1985 | 1986 | 1987 |

Indian Creek millage is 35.1270. Mean $/sf[4] = $67.15 × 1,401 [Subj sf] × 0.9[5] = $77,370 proper value. $98,500 less $77,370 = $21,000, rounded assessment reduction) × $.0351270 (mills) = **$738 tax dollars saved** from sales analysis.

[1] For our purposes, $98,500 is the county assessed value, not the sales price.
[2] Either adj or liv sf, but not both.
[3] The comparable sales must have occurred in the 12 months before 1/1/89.
[4] Mean = [Comp 1 $/sf + Comp 2 + Comp 3] ÷ 3.
[5] 10 percent sales cost reduction.

Congratulations! You have learned how to reduce your property taxes and you have the basic tools with which to do so.

# 5

## Your Case Support Materials

### Filling Out the Petition

State law governs the property tax appeal procedure and petition form items. The state law is derived from standardized national appraisal practices, such as the Federal National Mortgage Association (FNMA) appraisal form 1004 that you saw in the cases in Chapter 4; Federal Housing Administration (FHA) procedures; Federal Home Loan Mortgage Corporation (FHLMC), Federal Deposit Insurance Corporation (FDIC), and Resolution Trust Corporation (RTC) regulators, insurance company valuation standards, and national appraisal societies' methodology. Thus, there is little variation between California, New York, Texas, Florida, Illinois, and other states. A possible exception is a state with counties that have loosely enforced the state statute. These areas often have informal petition procedures.

Petition forms and instructions from states with over 95 percent of the U.S. population are presented in Chapter 6. Look for your state's form. We use the Dade County, Florida, petition form (Exhibit B) as an example here because it incorporates more information than many other forms. If your county has no form, you might want to use items from the Exhibit E form. This will give you an edge with the petition. The less organized your assessor is, the more likely you are to succeed and the greater is your potential assessment reduction. But **you must prepare your case carefully to maximize your chances for success.**

Below you will find explanations of potentially confusing petition items or the page number of your guide that answers the question.

Many of the answers to petition questions are on your **proposed tax notice, property tax roll printout, tax bill, warranty deed, and mortgage** (for example, the folio number, legal description, year built, assessment value, and millage).

## *Dade County Property Appraisal Adjustment Board (PAAB—like the BofE) Petition Form (Exhibit B)*

The upper left corner of the petition has a case **"agenda number."** The hearing notice will have your agenda number, folio number, date, time, and place of hearing.

### *Section 1 of PAAB/BofE Form*

**"Mail notices to OWNER"** (you). **AGENT** is a person employed by owner to appeal. You can employ yourself.

**"Amount of time requested."** Ten minutes is enough, or 15 minutes at most, unless you represent a condo association.

**"Have you discussed this petition with the Property Appraisal (Assessment) Officer?"** You only have two to six weeks (after you get your proposed tax bill) to file your petition, so you have to get your material together in the spring. Try to get a meeting in the spring or summer, before the September rush. If you can't schedule a meeting, get a note from the appraiser's office stating that you tried. Check "yes," and present the appraiser's note at the hearing.

The "INCOME APPROACH" does not apply to owner-occupied houses, unless many area dwellings are rentals.

Check box to get **"PROPERTY RECORD CARD."** We discussed this card previously. It shows livable and adjusted square footage, land, building assessments, and other information about your property.

### *Section 2*

**"Legal":** Sub(division), Happy Acres or Ft Dallas Sec 3. **"PB"** (Plat Book), often written PB 10/68 = book 10, page 68; X number of **"lots"** or **"parcels"** = a "Block"; 21 lots are in Block 1, 15 lots in Block 2; 5 or 10 blocks equal a "Subdivision."

**"Total Purchase Price"** is applicable only if purchased within last two years.

DADE COUNTY
**PROPERTY APPRAISAL ADJUSTMENT BOARD**
METRO-DADE CENTER, SUITE 1720
111 N.W. 1st STREET
MIAMI, FLORIDA 33128-1981

**AGENDA NUMBER**

**VERIFIED BY**

**PETITION FORM FOR 1989**

IMPORTANT NOTICE: A SEPARATE PETITION IS REQUIRED FOR EACH PARCEL OF PROPERTY (ie. EACH FOLIO NUMBER)
UNDER APPEAL, UNLESS PART OF A MULTIPLE FILING REQUIRING THE USE OF FORMS CIR/CT/PAAB 46 OR 47, AS INDICATED
IN SECTION 2 OF THIS PETITION. SEE BACK OF PERFORATED RECEIPT AT BOTTOM OF PETITION FOR FILING LOCATIONS.

**Phone 375-5641**

(PLEASE PRINT OR TYPE)   **THIS SECTION MUST BE COMPLETED BY ALL PETITIONERS**

PROPERTY OWNER'S NAME _____

MAIL NOTICES TO:  ☐ OWNER   ☐ AGENT (Name) _____

STREET ADDRESS _____ APT/SUITE NO. _____

CITY & STATE _____ ZIP CODE _____ (TEL.) HOME: _____ WORK: _____

Amount of time requested for hearing by Petitioner.....HOURS _____ MINUTES _____

If you are an eligible recipient of public assistance under Section 409.185, Florida Statutes, check box ☐. Obtain and submit copy of certificate of such eligibility issued by the Department of Health & Rehabilitative Services at time of filing, for waiver of filing fee.

Have you discussed this petition with the Property Appraiser's Office prior to filing this petition?   Yes ☐   No ☐...If no, any conference requested under F.S. 194.011(2) must be held prior to October 1, 1989.

Are you willing to submit additional information pertinent to this petition?  Yes ☐  No ☐   (NOTE: Documentation or income Data submitted in support of the "INCOME APPROACH" should be filed together with this petition or thereafter directly with the DADE COUNTY PROPERTY APPRAISER, Ste. 710, 111 NW 1 St., Miami 33128-1984, prior to date of hearing.) Petitioner submits the following information in support of this petition (include owner's name, the assessed value and description of any property adjacent to or of like nature, use and location of which comparison will show overassessment of the petitioner's property). However, if the comparable has an assessed value that is lower than its just value, the Board has no authority to lower petitioner's value based solely on the comparable property (attach addendum with supporting information). No petitioner may present, nor may the Board or Special Master accept, testimony or other evidentiary materials for consideration that were requested of the petitioner in writing by the Property Appraiser of which the petitioner had knowledge and denied to the Property Appraiser. (See Property Appraiser's letter on the reverse side of this page.)

It is anticipated all hearings for tax adjustments will be completed by January 31, 1990. Please indicate any date(s) when you will not be available to attend a hearing _____

Check box if petitioner requests that copy of property record card be furnished along with notice of hearing (agents must also file separate written authorization by petitioner for Property Appraiser to release confidential property record card containing confidential income information) ....... ☐

**②  COMPLETE THIS SECTION IF YOU ARE REQUESTING REVIEW OF ▶ REAL PROPERTY ASSESSMENTS**

| REAL PROPERTY FOLIO NO. | | | | | | | | | | | | | MULTIPLE FOLIO NUMBERS | USE FORM CIR/CT/PAAB 46 FOR CONDO, CO-OP & MOBILE HOME UNITS, OR FORM CIR/CT/PAAB 47 FOR OTHER TYPES OF CONTIGUOUS PROPERTIES. |

LEGAL DESCRIPTION: SUB _____ PB _____ LOT _____ BLK _____

STREET ADDRESS _____ CITY _____ DATE PURCHASED: _____

ASSESSED VALUE $ _____ PETITIONER'S ESTIMATE OF VALUE $ _____

TYPE OF PROPERTY (Check Appropriate Box):
☐ Residential  ☐ Duplex  ☐ Apt. Bldg.  ☐ Condo  ☐ Motel  ☐ Hotel  ☐ Office  ☐ Store  ☐ Shopping Center
☐ Industrial  ☐ Vacant  ☐ Agriculture  Other (Describe) _____

ANSWER THE FOLLOWING QUESTIONS, IF APPLICABLE:
Total Purchase Price $ _____ Land Cost $ _____ Bldg. Cost $ _____ Date Built _____
Improvement Cost (After Purchase) $ _____ Amount of Insurance Carried on Property $ _____
Date of Mortgage (If any) _____ Initial Mortgage $ _____ Current Balance Due $ _____
Check box if appeal is based in whole or in part on the fact that the improvements were not substantially complete as of Jan. 1, 1989....☐
Was Certificate of Occupancy issued prior to January 1, 1989? _____ Yes ☐ No ☐
Is Property Rented or Leased?  ☐ Yes  ☐ No  Gross Income $ _____ Net Income $ _____
Professional Appraisal Value $ _____
If a Condominium, is it an individual Unit?  ☐ Yes  ☐ No
If Condo Owned by Developer, indicate the Total Number of Condo Units Constructed _____ Date Built _____
Number of Condo Units Unsold _____
List All Folio Numbers of those Condo Units included in this Appeal (Use Form CIR/CT/PAAB 46, SCHEDULE OF MULTIPLE UNITS) and File as Attachment to this Petition.

**③  COMPLETE THIS SECTION IF YOU ARE REQUESTING REVIEW OF ▶ PERSONAL PROPERTY**

| PERSONAL PROPERTY FOLIO NO. | | | | | | | |

Business Name _____
Address _____
Assessed Value $ _____ Estimated Value $ _____
Describe Operations _____ Date Started _____
Acquisition Date(s) Furniture/Fixtures/Equipment _____ Cost $ _____ (Attach schedule if necessary)
Amount of personal property, mortgaged or pledged as security for debt $ _____ Date _____
Balance Due $ _____ Amount of Insurance on Furniture/Fixtures/Equipment $ _____
Professional Appraisal Value $ _____ Dated _____

**◆  REVIEW OF EXEMPTIONS   OR   AGRICULTURE CLASSIFICATIONS**

**ALL PARTIES SEEKING REVIEW OF DENIAL OF NON—HOMESTEAD EXEMPTIONS OR AGRICULTURE CLASSIFICATIONS** should have previously filed separate petition form CIR/CT/PAAB-45. The statutory deadline for the filing of such form was **JULY 31, 1989** and, therefore, taxpayers who have not yet filed cannot be granted a hearing by the Board. Petitions for review of Homestead Exemption may still be filed on form CIR/CT/PAAB 50 on or before September 18, 1989 or such other date as may be designated on the notice of proposed property taxes.

**◆  NOTARIZE THIS SECTION**

State of Florida, County of Dade, before me, the undersigned authority, personally appeared _____
Who in my presence subscribed the foregoing petition and who after being duly sworn deposed and said that he is the owner, or authorized agent of the owner, of the property described in the foregoing petition and that the above and foregoing statements of matters, facts and exhibits attached hereto are true and correct, this _____ day of _____ 1989.

PETITIONER'S
SIGNATURE _____  NOTARY PUBLIC (Or Deputy Clerk) _____
                            MY COMMISSION EXPIRES _____ 19___.

**(NOTE:** If AGENT other than an ATTORNEY, CERT. PUBLIC ACCOUNTANT or REGISTERED REAL ESTATE BROKER, has been designated to file this petition and represent the owner, written confirmation of such agency, signed and attested by owner, should be attached and filed with petition.)

**◆  DO NOT WRITE BELOW THIS LINE**

I hereby certify that the foregoing petition to the Property Appraisal Adjustmen. Board was filed with the undersigned clerk of the governing body of this County on the _____ day of _____ 1989 at _____ (AM, PM) and the signing and delivery of a copy by me to the petitioner constitutes a receipt. I further certify that a copy of the foregoing petition was furnished by me to the Property Appraiser of this County.

_____
Deputy Clerk

CIR/CT/PAAB 43 Rev. 8/89 METRO-DADE/GSA-MAT

**"Date Built"** is 19XX.

**"Improvement cost after purchase"** requires copies of all receipts and estimates. Remember, this does not include personal property.

**"Amount of insurance carried on property."** Submit policy cover page and amount of insurance. Fill in the mortgage information.

**"Was Certificate of Occupancy issued prior to Jan 1, 1990?"** If issued after January 1, you may not be liable for any taxes for the year, or liable only for prorated taxes based on the date of certificate of occupancy (CO) issuance.

**"Rented or leased?"** If yes, you have income-producing property, and will need a rental survey, an income approach, and a comparable sales analysis beyond the scope of this book.

**"Professional Appraisal Value"** done by a certified appraiser, licensed by the state. The 1980s S&L real estate debacle was due in part to inflated appraisal values. In the near future, appraisals will be free of the real estate broker profession.

## Section 3

**Folio Number.** This is the most important identification number your property has. Sometimes your **proposed tax bill** is printed in such a way that the last integer is missing, or perhaps the last two. For example, "23456789" may be printed "234567," the 89 being off the page. You can tell by checking the number of blank squares on the **appeals form.** Does it conform to your folio number? If not, look on your old tax bills on your lender's monthly invoice, on your deed, and on your mortgage.

**Warranty Deed.** This is the document you signed to buy your property. If you bought it within the last two years, it has direct bearing on your appeal. To impress the special master, it would help to photocopy at least the most relevant pages of the deed and mortgage, with the sale price, mortgage amount, and any relevant clauses. If you bought your house more than 2.5 years ago, the sale is irrelevant because the market has changed.

**Mortgage.** See the section of Chapter 2 on mortgages.

## Section 4

Section 4 is not applicable.

## *Sections 5 and 6*

**"Notarized signature."** The appraiser office clerk is usually a notary.
RECEIPT.
"X" the "Property Owner"; put in the folio number.
Read the checklist on the right side of the petition.

# 6

# State-by-State Analysis

From conversations with the tax appeal agents, assessors and court clerks all over the United States, the author formed impressions about the degree of ease or difficulty of obtaining a tax reduction. These impressions are summed up to the right of the name of the state. This guide should give a petitioner the benefit of any doubt. For example, if the reader sees "good program" by his state name, it means that using the guide gives him a good chance of obtaining a reduction. Those states which are not listed do not use official forms, but their procedures are much the same as neighboring states.

## ALABAMA (Fair to Good Program)

The Parcel Identification Number is the folio number. Note 9 states that you need not be present to obtain a reduction. Most states will not consider an appeal unless the petitioner or his representative is present at the hearing.

## ARIZONA (Good Program)

You have a very fair tax tribunal system in a sophisticated property tax appeal state. Relief may be granted at any of the following steps, eliminating the need to pursue the case further. Step one is to file a petition with the county assessor's office. Step two, the second appeal, is to the county board of equalization. Step three is to appeal to the state board of tax appeals. Before any step, the taxpayer may appeal **directly** to superior court. Evidence the taxpayer presents could be the basis of either increasing or decreasing the taxpayer's property tax.

## ARKANSAS (Difficult Program)

Arkansas seems to be one of the more difficult states in which to obtain tax relief. However, this situation is mitigated by the fact that Arkansas has no appeal forms. The procedure is to:

1. Write a letter to the county clerk.
2. If not satisfied, to go the BofE.
3. Appeal to the county executive officer, in Arkansas called "county judge."
4. Appeal to circuit court, then to the Arkansas supreme court.

## CALIFORNIA (Excellent Program)

Californians are well-educated tax-wise, and the county assessment appeals board (BofE) is very responsive to inequities. The BofE does require petitioner presence at the informal hearing. Nonappearance will result in denial of the application. When the petition concerns recently purchased property, comparable sales must have occurred **no less than 90 days** after the date of transfer or purchase. (The California market is so volatile that six- or nine-month-old comparable sales would not reflect the value of the subject property.)

## COLORADO (Good Program)

Colorado is another progressive state where property tax is concerned. After seeing the county property assessor, the petitioner appeals to the county commissioners, sitting as the BofE. Next the petitioner may file with the state board of assessment appeals or district court, or the taxpayer may request binding arbitration. The last two steps are to appeal to Colorado appeals court, and finally, to the Colorado supreme court.

Colorado's petition for abatement or refund of taxes is ratified by the county commission. The final ratification is the state property tax administrator's responsibility. (Note: Some tax information, other than ad valorem, is included for the taxpayer's benefit.)

## CONNECTICUT (Good Program)

This state is responsive to taxpayer (voter!) assessment problems. The board of tax review form states that the CD, or coefficient of dispersion, is 100 percent, meaning that the assessed value is 100 percent of the market value. The taxpayer or his proxy must be present to obtain a hearing. This form is straightforward, but supporting material must be included (recent comparables and so forth).

## DELAWARE (Good Program)

The board of assessment review allows you or your agent to present your case, or allows you to present your documented, completed form to be analyzed and acted upon by the board in your absence, should you so desire.

Rules of hearsay apply: the taxpayer's appraisal must be presented by the appraiser in person; expert witnesses must present expert evidence, should you desire a hearing.

## FLORIDA (Excellent Program)

First, discuss your case with your county assessor or appeals board, then appeal to your county BofE, then to the circuit court, and finally to the Florida supreme court. Florida counties have different names for the BofE.

## GEORGIA (Good Process)

Georgia has no formal appeal forms; a letter of petition is all that is required. This means that when you follow this guide's instructions, your chances of relief are excellent. Georgia's appeal process is:

1. Write a letter of appeal to your county tax assessor.
2. Appeal to your county board of equalization.
3. Appeal to superior court (circuit court). Superior court may review the BofE findings.

## HAWAII (Very Good Program)

After receiving his proposed tax notice, a Hawaiian property owner first sees his county assessor representative. If not satisfied he files with his county board of review. If still unsatisfied, he appeals to the clerk of the tax appeals court in Honolulu. There are time limits and opportunities for pretrial conferences, and a fee schedule ranging from $5 to $100.

### IDAHO (Fair Program)

Although Idaho is not the easiest state in the union in which to obtain tax relief, Idahoans can take refuge in the programmed steps to relief outlined in this book.

### ILLINOIS (Excellent Program)

A very detailed and educational format, lending itself to relatively quick relief. Note on page 2 of the "Welcome to the Board of Appeals" brochure residential property is assessed at 16 percent of market value. Page 3's "Grounds for Appeal" (Ground 1) allows assessment relief for "property receiving a lower assessment than you." The Cook County "Lack of Uniformity" flyer gives instructions you should follow if this is your case. The appeals board may take the position that your neighbor's lower assessment is a mistake, and your higher assessment is the correct one. Stand your ground. Remember, this is an adversarial process. You have scored. So if you find your property is assessed higher than your similar neighbor's (or neighbors') lower assessment(s), photocopy the Illinois brochure and get that reduced assessment. This argument will often stand alone, and it will support other arguments for relief. The BofE's very reason for existence is to **equalize tax assessments.**

Page 4 of the brochure mentions square feet of living area and lot size. If the appraiser has allotted you more square footage than you actually have, your case is strong.

### INDIANA (Good Program)

This board of review's excellent, precise, detailed form includes two columns on the right side of the page, each with an "Agree" or "Disagree" indication. It makes for ease of (justified) tax relief. One column is for the township assessor and the other is for the board of review. The form is very clear, allowing the taxpayer the opportunity to briefly, clearly, and pointedly present his situation to the relief authorities.

## IOWA (Good Program)

The "Assessor's Duties" brochure flow chart provides a good picture of how the tax rate and the taxpayer bill are prepared. The relationship between the market value and the assessed value is not clear, but the assessed value—net taxable value—is clear.

## KANSAS (Good Program)

The state board of tax appeals form is first used with the county assessor; second, with the hearing officer or panel or the county commissioners (if available), and finally with the SBTA itself. In Kansas, unlike most states, the taxpayer may appeal tax assessments and payments several years old.

## KENTUCKY (Good Program)

The county board of assessment appeals (BofE) hears cases after the county assessor (actually the property valuation administrator) has conferred with the tax petitioner. Only one member of the board shall have extensive knowledge of real estate values. The two other members shall be of "business or farming" background.

## LOUISIANA (Fair to Good Program)

Louisiana has a two-week public inspection of assessment lists, in August and September. Board of review (BofE) determination must accompany the appeal to the Louisiana tax commission. At the informal hearing, modified rules of evidence of the district court apply.

## MAINE (Good to Fair Program)

This is a relatively simple form, which captures the gist of good property tax reduction methodology.

## MARYLAND (Good Program)

This appeal form, on the back of the notice of assessment, puts the burden of proof as well as the data gathering and presentation up to the taxpayer.

## MASSACHUSETTS (Excellent Program)

Massachusetts has an appeals procedure for level one, at the county assessor's office. Those dissatisfied with their decision may appeal to the appellate tax board, filing the proper appeal through the appropriate channels.

The homestead (owner) exemption and quite a few other exemptions and tax deferments are described in the "FY 1990 Tax Bill Problem" resolution brochure.

## MICHIGAN (Good but Tough Program)

Assessment protest begins with a protest to the local county board review. After this, the homestead petitioner ($25 filing fee) may request a hearing in the small claims division of tax court, or petitioner may appeal directly to the tax tribunal. The taxpayer has a right to a rehearing, should he desire it, and has the options of appealing up through the Michigan supreme court. A very thorough Michigan tax tribunal guide is included for reference. The "Small Claims Division Petition Form" is deceptively simple. Make sure you include data discussed in this guide. Protests dating back several years are allowed under guidelines specified in the brochure reprinted.

## MINNESOTA (Good Program)

The first appeal level is the Minnesota tax court, similar to the BofE. However, the tax court has two divisions: the small claims division (filing fee $2) handles matters under $5,000, and this court's decision is final. The regular division (filing fee $25) of the tax court handles matters involving $5,000 or more. Petitioners dissatisfied with the results of this procedure, whose disputed bill sum exceeds $5,000, may appeal to a Minnesota superior court.

## MISSISSIPPI (Fair to Good Program)

The county board of supervisors acts as the BofE. Appeal essentials are on the one-page abbreviated form.

## MISSOURI (Good to Fair Program)

The BofE may lower, raise, or keep the present tax assessment. The taxpayer or his agent may present the case. Three or four nearby recent comparable sales can be presented.

## NEBRASKA (Fair Program)

County BofE is appeal of second resort (after county assessor). Nebraska tax commissioner receives a copy of the findings.

## NEW JERSEY (Good Program)

The first three quarters (75 percent) of a homeowner's taxes for the year being appealed must be **paid** before the hearing. A New Jerseyan's first appeal is to his county board of taxation. Dissatisfied appellants may file a further appeal to the tax court of New Jersey in Trenton.

## NEW MEXICO (Fair to Good Program)

If your petition (protest) has not been acted upon by December 5 or thereabouts, you are required to remit half of the unprotested amount (property owner's amount) by that date.

## NEW YORK (Excellent Program)

The BofE (county board of assessment review, or, in smaller counties, the county assessor) does not require a personal appearance at the review, but such an appearance is recommended. You will not be able to obtain more than your requested reduction, even if data support a greater reduction. Should you appeal your decision to small claims, superior, or state supreme court, you may also be precluded from obtaining a greater reduction than that requested. Note the Long Island form.

## OHIO (Very Good Program)

The county board of revision may increase or decrease the total value of a parcel included in a complaint. Evidence as to valuation must include the total value of land and buildings. The overassessment of land coupled with the underassessment of buildings will not justify a reduction.

## OKLAHOMA (Fair Program)

The petition form is simple, but this means you have a fairly good chance to obtain relief. Go for it!

## OREGON  (Fair to Good Program)

Step 1 is to discuss the assessment with your assessor. Step 2 is to file a petition with the county BofE by May 31. Step 3 is to appeal this decision to the small claims court or the Oregon department of revenue. The department of revenue will consider appeals for the current tax year **plus the two previous years!**

## PENNSYLVANIA  (Very Good Program)

Note the capital expenditure section (Section 2). Your receipts, estimates, and so forth should be included in your presentation.

## SOUTH CAROLINA  (Fair Program)

The review of assessment may result in no change or in a decreased or increased assessment. Count your beans.

## TENNESSEE  (Good Program)

Your board of equalization forms include separate land and improvements (buildings). You may choose to allow the BofE to determine your assessment relief without a hearing.

## TEXAS  (Excellent Program)

The appraisal review board (BofE) recognizes incorrect property descriptions, incorrect owner names, and failure to send required notice as reasons to obtain relief.

## UTAH  (Fair to Good Program)

The BofE has the power to raise or lower your assessment, based upon the facts presented. This tends to preclude protesting land and excluding buildings.

## VIRGINIA  (Very Good Program)

The BofE (called the department of real estate assessments) has the power to raise or lower assessments.

## WASHINGTON (Very Good Program)

Property is assessed at 100 percent of market value. Step 1 is to collect your data and set up an appointment with a county assessor or appraiser. Step 2 is either to file a complaint in superior court (with an attorney) or to file a petition with the county BofE, using the form provided. You should request and review the material that the county assessor will present to refute (or support!) your petition. Attendance at this informal hearing is optional, but you should attend. The first half year's taxes should be paid by April 30 to avoid interest and penalty charges. Step 3 is to appeal the county board's decision to the state board of tax appeals. Step 4 is to appeal the latter decision to superior court.

## WISCONSIN (Good Program)

The formal objection to a real estate assessment includes questions about fire insurance, repairs and improvements of the property, how long the property took to sell if sold in the past five years, and appraisal value. You must include the hard copy (receipts, estimates, insurance policies) in your presentation. It wouldn't hurt to include your Schedule A (mortgage payments).

# 7

# *Journal Articles, Federal and State Court Property Appeal Summaries*

Some of the articles bear only peripherally on property tax reduction; others directly. Scan them to determine their value to you.

## *Journal Articles*

"**Selling a Residence: Current Opportunities for Deferring or Eliminating the Tax on Gain,**" by Melvin Marder and Calvin Engler, *Taxation for Accountants,* vol. 36, June 1986, p. 348(b). Taxes on the sale of residential dwellings can be deferred, under Section 1034 of the IRS Code, when the home seller is less than 55 years of age. However, the seller must also buy a replacement dwelling. Section 121 allows the taxpayer to protect as much as $125,000 from a realized gain.

"**Your Home: Time to Cash in on All That Equity?**" *Medical Economics,* vol. 65, Oct. 24, 1988, p. 132(6).

"**Purchase and Ownership of a Residence Can Provide Many Tax Saving Opportunities,**" by Mindy P. Hupp, *Taxation for Accountants,* vol. 38, April 1987, p. 218(6). Tax savings arising from home ownership are discussed. "Points" paid on a home loan (mortgage) are totally deductible from gross income in the year of the purchase (Schedule A, Interest Expenses, Item 10, Deductible Points). Interest paid on mortgage and home improvement loans are deductible. Real property taxes paid in the year of sale are deductible in some states, if the taxes are paid when the payer did not occupy the home. Closing costs, recording fees, title expenses, and transfer taxes paid upon purchase of the home may be added to its value when the home is sold, to reduce the amount of gain from the sale, and thus save taxes. Home improvement costs should be added to the value of the home to reduce the gain upon its sale. Other tax advantages are discussed relative to condo purchases, use of the home as an office, home rental, and form of ownership elected (joint tenancy, tenancy in common, or tenancy by entirety).

**"The Case for Reform of the Real Property Tax,"** by John M. Kelly, *The American Journal of Economics and Sociology,* vol. 46, Jan. 1987, p. 125(2).

**"Real Estate Assessment Uniformity in Illinois,"** by J. Fred Giertz and David L. Chicoine, *Illinois Business Review,* vol. 45, Feb. 1988, p. 12(4).

**"Loading for Taxes** (for the independent fee appraiser),'' by Root H. Gerhardt, *Real Estate Appraiser & Analyst,* vol. 51, Fall 1985, p. 47(4). This article identifies creative financing as a distorting element in the real value of a home. Assessors may not pick up on this. Example: The sale price may represent an exaggerated future value as an important element of the sale price. The present value may be much lower. Such a comparable inflates the real, present worth of the property.

## *Property Appeal Cases, Identified by Topics, That May Help You Prepare Your Case*

The material referred to below is from Corpus Juris Secundum, vol. 84, pp. 998 ff, & Supplement, pp. 165 ff. The Supplement refers to a page in vol. 84, and this page is also quoted. The footnotes (FN) go from 1 to 99, then start over again. The Corpus text footnotes are also numbered 1–99. Corpus Juris Secundum is a legal textbook which is available in public libraries everywhere. It's written in a relatively easy-to-read style, even for non-lawyers.

### Legal Background of Homeowner Property Tax Appeal.

Look for footnote headings that may affect your property tax petition. Then look up the footnote. If that footnote is from your state, or a neighboring state, you hit the jackpot! If the state is near yours, it's almost as good. Even if the state is distant, it will be an asset.

We lack the space to print the abstracts, much less the opinions, that the footnotes refer to. But you can obtain any case decision and opinion from a large law firm library, or from a university law library. If you have a relative or friend who is a lawyer, ask him or her to photocopy the case or abstract for you.

The legal concept of **constructive notice** allows you to use the case material not only when you submit your petition and supporting material to the BofE, but also at the prehearing conference and at the hearing itself. Constructive notice is notice given by the public record. These are the legal and other notices you see in your local newspapers, community papers, and legal review newspapers. The law presumes that everyone has the same knowledge of all instruments that are properly recorded, as if everyone were actually acquainted with them.

### Creation and Organization of Board of Office of Property Appeals.

In General (Corpus Juris Secundum, p. 992, footnotes, or FN 93–99 and 1–18; CJS Supplement, p. 166, p. 998, FN 93–97; 1–30).

Creation of Board, FN 30–34; Board Composition, FN 35–43; Board Member Qualifications, FN 44–92.

Assessment review boards are considered to be public boards, and their members public officers. In some jurisdictions, the organization and existence of such boards are the subject of state constitutional provision. In this case, the boards are recognized constitutional bodies with corresponding status. When the state constitution allows the matter of assessment to be legislated, the lawmakers may create boards of assessment review (BofEs) or dismantle them. This power is not abrogated by a constitutional provision that tax assessors be elected.

When the constitution requires county assessment review officers to be elected, they may not be appointed. Otherwise they may be appointed by county executives or by other authorized public officials.

Generally, where ex officio members of the tax review board are members of another similar (or dissimilar) board, the two boards are distinct and separate. This holds in spite of organizational similarity and personnel identity. However, this does not disallow several boards merging, or (a) board(s) relinquishing its responsibility and authority to a new board, as long as this process follows legislative mandate.

Legislation may allow different types of BofEs in different parts of the state, as long as there is equality and uniformity in taxation. It also follows that different types of BofEs may be established for residential, multifamily, commercial, and industrial property. When a board consists of three members, the absence of one does not invalidate a decision made by the other two (a majority), who make up a quorum.

## Correction of Errors and Mistakes.

The BofEs or other officials charged with equalization of ad valorem taxes may not exceed their statutory limits in granting relief. Such corrections usually include mathematical error, property owner names, and legal description of the property. The BofE or officer does have the authority to directly correct ministerial error, or to order the error corrected.

A County BofE can correct its own (county assessment) errors, but not a state tax board error. It cannot retroactively correct error after a year's work has ended. For example, the BofE cannot partially refund 1990 property tax to a 1991 tax petitioner.

When the BofE's authority has been limited to clerical error, then fundamental error of substance, judgment, and law is not in the BofE's purview. However, it has been held that clerical error, where this distinction prevails, is not limited to mistakes that occur in copying or in mathematics.

Fundamental error concerns the basis of a tax, defects in the tax law, and assessor/BofE error acting within the aegis of their authority. Conversely, errors made by assessors/BofE acting outside the bounds of their mandate are subject to correction as clerical error. Under still other statutes, errors involving judgment or discretion are outside the purview of the assessor's/ BofE's authority to correct.

## Error Not Apparent on Tax Roll.

Some BofE/assessors are limited to correcting errors evident on the face of the tax roll, while other BofE are empowered to redress all error where assessor judgment is not involved.

## Time Limits of Correction Period (Footnotes 19–28).

Correction of assessment error is restricted to the current tax correction year. It is not retroactive (that is, for past years; when 1991 tax cases are being heard, 1990 error cannot be corrected). But when the assessment is made in odd-numbered years, a BofE can correct assessments in an even-numbered year.

## Reduction and Reassessment (Footnotes 1–78).

BofE (review boards) may reduce assessments if so mandated.

In Idaho, Illinois, Iowa, Michigan, Nebraska, New Jersey, North Dakota, Ohio, Texas, and Washington, the BofE has the power to reduce and (in some of these states) to increase assessments. In North Dakota the BofE's authority to reduce assessments requires the concurrence of certain other officials.

When county commissioners obtain under-market-value property via tax deed, the sale does not necessarily constitute a good comparable sale (SD).

**For more detailed information . . .**

**Change of Valuation or Amount of Tax** (In General, Increase, Reduction (CJS, p. 1008, FN 37–65); CJS Supplement, p. 166, p. 1008, FN 37–99; 1–42).

**Increase in Assessment** (FN 66–99); Reduction (FN 1–42; CJS Supplement, p. 166, p. 1008, FN 37–99; 1–42).

**Reduction** (CJS, p. 1014, FN 1–42; CJS Supplement, p. 167, 1–42).

**Reassessment** (CJS, p. 1017, FN 43–78; CJS Supplement, p. 167, p. 1017, FN 43–73).

**Notice of Public Meeting** (CJS, p. 1021, FN 99; 1–8).

**Time and Place for Objections or Application for Review** (CJS, p. 1021, FN 9–22; CJS Supplement, p. 167, FN 9–22).

**Proceedings** (CJS, p. 1023, FN 23–35; CJS Supplement, p. 168, p. 1023, FN 23–60).

**Complaint, Petition or Application for Review** (FN 36–74; CJS Supplement, 169, p. 1032, FN 36–67).

**Notice to Persons Interested** (CJS, p. 1026, FN 52–76; CJS Supplement, p. 168, FN 52–76).

**Persons Notified** (CJS, p. 1030, FN 13–23; CJS Supplement, p. 169, FN 13–23).

**Waiver or Objections to Notice** (CJS, p. 1031, FN 24–35; CJS Supplement, p. 169, FN 24–35).

**Answer and Reply** (CJS, p. 1035, FN 75–78; CJS Supplement, p. 169, FN 75–95).

**Evidence** (CJS, p. 1036, FN 79–93; CJS Supplement, p. 170, FN 79–93).

**Admissibility** (CJS, pp. 1037–38, FN 94–99, CJS Supplement, p. 170, p. 1037, FN under "Evidence Held Admissible/Not Admissible," FN 98–99).

**Hearsay Evidence** (CJS, p. 1038, FN 96–98).

**Weight and Sufficiency** (CJS, p. 1039, FN 5–32; CJS Supplement, p. 170, FN 5–32).

**Taxpayer's Witnesses** (CJS Supplement, p. 172, FN 11–31).

**Hearing** (CJS, p. 1042, FN 33–74; CJS Supplement, p. 170, FN 33–70).

**Judgment or Decision and Record** (CJS, p. 1045, FN 76–81; CJS Supplement, FN 76–81).

**Decision Based Upon Evidence at Hand** (CJS, p. 1040, FN 16–32; CJS Supplement, p. 172, FN 16–32). Ordinarily, a hearing is conducted to facilitate both sides' presentations so as to render a decision conforming to justice and the statutes (CJS, p. 1042, FN 33–66; CJS Supplement, p. 172, FN 33–66).

**Board Determination** (CJS, p. 1045, FN 75–81; CJS Supplement, p. 173, p. 1045, FN 76–80).

**Degree of Relief Allowed** (CJS p. 1046, FV 82–93; CJS Supplement, p. 173, pp. 1046, FN 82–86).

**The Decision: Its Form, Requisites, Execution** (CJS, p. 1046, FN 94–99; 1–16; CJS Supplement, p. 173, p. 1047, FN 94–99; 1–30).

## *Exhibit A1.*

**Tax Reduction Data for Tax Appeal Hearing.**

|  | Subject | Comp 1 | Comp 2 | Comp 3 |
|---|---|---|---|---|
| **Address** | _____ | _____ | _____ | _____ |
| **Sales price** | _____ [1] | _____ | _____ | _____ |
| **Sq ft** | _____ | _____ | _____ | _____ |
| **$___/sf** | _____ | _____ | _____ | _____ |
| **Lot size** | _____ | _____ | _____ | _____ |
| **Sale Date** | _____ | _____ | _____ | _____ |
| **Bd/Ba** | _____ | _____ | _____ | _____ |
| **Dist from subj** | _____ | _____ | _____ | _____ |
| **Yr blt** | _____ | _____ | _____ | _____ |

$X\$/sf^2 = \$$ _____ $\div 3 \times$ _____ [Subj sf] $\times 0.9^3 = \$$ _____ proper value.
$\$$ _____ less $\$$ _____ $= \$$ _____ assessment reduction $\times .0$ _____ (mills) $= \$$ _____ tax saving from sales analysis.

[1] $\$$ _____ is the assessed value, not the sales price.

[2] Mean $=$ [Comp 1 $/sf + Comp 2 + Comp 3] $\div 3 =$ _____ $\$/sf =$
$\$$ _____ $\div 3 \times$ [Subj sf] $\times 0.9 = \$$ _____ proper value. $\$$ _____ less
$\$$ _____ $= \$$ _____ assessment reduction $\times .0$ _____ [mills] $= \$$ _____ tax saving from sales analysis.

[3] Ten percent sales costs deductible.

## *Exhibit A2.*

**Tax Reduction Data for Tax Appeal Hearing.**

|  | Subject | Comp 1 | Comp 2 | Comp 3 |
|---|---|---|---|---|
| **Address** | _____ | _____ | _____ | _____ |
| **Sales price** | _____ [1] | _____ | _____ | _____ |
| **Sq ft** | _____ | _____ | _____ | _____ |
| **$___/sf** | _____ | _____ | _____ | _____ |
| **Lot size** | _____ | _____ | _____ | _____ |
| **Sale date** | _____ | _____ | _____ | _____ |
| **Bd/Ba** | _____ | _____ | _____ | _____ |
| **Dist from subj** | _____ | _____ | _____ | _____ |
| **Yr blt** | _____ | _____ | _____ | _____ |

Mean\$/sf$^2$ = \$ _____ ÷ 3 × [Subj sf] × $0.9^3$ = \$ _____ proper value. \$ _____ less \$ _____ = \$ _____ assessment reduction × .0 _____ (mills) = \$ _____ tax saving from sales analysis.
$^3$ Ten percent sales costs deductible.

**Record of Proceedings** (CJS, p. 1048, FN 17–34; CJS Supplement, p. 174, FN 17–34).

**Conclusiveness and Effect of Decision** (CJS, p. 1050, FN 35–78; CJS Supplement, p. 174–75, p. 1055, FN 79–93).

**Mode of Correction** (CJS, p. 1054, FN 79–98; CJS Supplement, p. 172, FN 79–87).

**Review or Reverse by Superior Officer, Board, or Authority** (CJS, p. 1056, FN 4–98).

**Court Review** (CJS, p. 1064, FN 99; 1–18).

**Appeal; Certiori** (CJS Supplement, p. 176, p. 1064, FN 99; 1–29).

## *Exhibit A3.*

**Tax Reduction Data or Tax Appeal Hearing.**

|  | Subject | Comp 1 | Comp 2 | Comp 3 |
|---|---|---|---|---|
| **Address** | _____ | _____ | _____ | _____ |
| **Sales price** | _____ [1] | _____ | _____ | _____ |
| **Sq ft** | _____ | _____ | _____ | _____ |
| **$___/sf** | _____ | _____ | _____ | _____ |
| **Lot size** | _____ | _____ | _____ | _____ |
| **Sale date** | _____ | _____ | _____ | _____ |
| **Bd/Ba** | _____ | _____ | _____ | _____ |
| **Dist from subj** | _____ | _____ | _____ | _____ |
| **Yr blt** | _____ | _____ | _____ | _____ |

Mean$/sf[2] = $ ____ ÷ × ____ [Subj sf] × $0.9^3$ = $ ____ proper
value. $ ____ less $ ____ = $ ____ assessment reduction × .0
[mills] = $ ____
                        tax saving from sales analysis.
[1] $ ____ is the assessed value, not the sales price.
[2] Mean = [Comp 1 $/sf + Comp 2 + Comp 3] ÷ 3 = ____ $/sf =
$ ____ ÷ 3 × ____ [Subj sf] × .9 = $ ____ proper value.
$ ____ less $ ____ = $ ____ assessment reduction × .0 ____ [mills] =
$ ____ tax saving from sales analysis.
[3] Ten percent costs deductible.

# 8

# Tax Reduction Vocabulary

You can accelerate your learning process by learning this tax reduction vocabulary.

**Abatement**   An official reduction or cessation of an assessed valuation for ad valorem taxation after the initial assessment has been completed.

**Abstraction method** (similar to allocation and extraction)   The allocation of the appraised total value of the property between land and building. This may be accomplished either on a ratio basis or by subtracting a figure representing building value from the appraised total value of the property. Although a distribution or allocation of a price or value between land improvements by statistical ratios can be useful at times, the procedure has limitations.

**Abut**   to touch or border upon, as a residential lot abutting a commercially zoned area, for example, a shopping center.

**A/C**   Air conditioning.

**Accessibility**
1. The relative degree of effort (time and cost) by which a site can be reached. A relative term used to indicate ease of entrance upon a property.
2. A location factor that will implement the most probable profitable use of a site in terms of ease and convenience.

**Actual age**   How many years old is the structure? Often expressed as the year the house was built. The number of years elapsed since an original structure was built. Historical or chronological age.

**Adjusted basis**   The original cost of a property plus allowable additions, including capital improvements, certain carrying costs, and assessments minus allowed depreciation and partial sales.

**Adjusted square feet**   Often your folio-Pin card/printout in the assessor's office will list your "Adjusted Square Feet" (adj sf, asf). This is distinct from your **living** square feet, but your **adjusted square feet includes your living square feet.** Look at the most common formula for adjusting square feet, in Figure 2-4.

**Adjustments**

1. *Net*—Those figures that are added to or subtracted from the sales prices of comparable properties to obtain an adjusted sales price of each comparable property. The result is the appraiser's best estimate of what each comparable property would have sold for if it had possessed all of the salient characteristics of the subject property.

2. *Dollar*—The identification of individual differences between comparable sales and the subject property in terms of plus or minus dollar amounts. To obtain an adjusted sales price for the comparable properties (not the subject property) for the differences identified.

3. *Percentage*—The identification of individual differences between comparable sales and the subject property in terms of plus or minus percentage differentials. Individual percentage adjustments are then summed and converted to dollar amounts based upon the sales price of the comparable in order to form the net adjustment.

4. *Cumulative Percentage*—the identification of individual differences between comparable sales and the subject property in terms of plus or minus percentage differentials, cumulating them by multiplication or division. The process assumes a causal relationship among the various factors for which adjustments were made; that is, it carries the implication that there is correlation among the factors. Cumulative percentage adjustments are not recommended.

**Ad valorem tax**   Literally, "to the value." For our purposes, ad valorem tax means property tax.

**Allocation** (similar to abstraction, extraction)   To estimate the value of your lot, or site, **only,** without the improvements (as an empty lot):

1. Find the recent sales of vacant lots in your (or similar) neighborhood.

2. Find recent sales of homes in your (or similar) neighborhood.

3. Dividing item 1 by item 2 yields a percentage indicating the value of your unimproved lot.

Example: Three vacant lots in areas similar to yours selling for an average of $20,000. You find three comparables (houses like yours) selling for an average of $80,000: $20,000 ÷ $80,000 = 25 percent. You check with your county assessor to find that your area assessments are supposed to be 100 percent of the market value. Your total assessment (lot plus improvement, or building) is $80,000. Your lot is assessed at $36,000 and your house at $44,000 (for a total of $80,000). Therefore, $80,000 ÷ 0.9 = $88,900 (rounded) market value of your house and lot.

| *Comparables* | *Your house* |
|---|---|
| Recent sale price $80,000 | Not sold |
| Vacant site sales $20,000 | Not sold |
| 25 percent lot allocation $20,000 | |
| Your lot assessment | $36,000 |

Although your total assessment is in line with the comparables, the 25 percent allocation to similar lots indicates a value of **$20,000,** rather than your tax bill's $36,000, a $13,000 lot **overassessment.** So you appeal the **lot only, because the improvement (house) is underassessed.** In your petition, you clearly state a request for a lot-**assessment-only** hearing. As the special master rarely has the power to **raise** assessments, you can win. Sometimes, however, the assessor will say that the distinction doesn't mean anything, only the total assessment counts. Your position, of course, is that the separate items indicate there is a distinction, and on this basis you have a right to a $13,000 reduction. You should not be held liable (taxable) for the assessor's error.

**Appraisal**   An estimate or opinion of value. The act or process of estimating value. This value opinion may be oral or written. Usually it is a written document.

**Appraisal date**   Date on appraisal; usually renders appraisal usable for six months.

**Appraisal methods**   Approaches used in real property appraisal: (1) cost analysis (how much to erect a similar building); (2) comparative sales analysis, also called direct sales comparison, or market data analysis; (3) income analysis, if the property is income producing. A more scientific but as yet less accurate appraisal method is **multivariate analysis.**

**Appraisal report**   In residential appraisals, usually the FNMA 1004 Form with pictures, maps locating subject and comparables, sketch of the building, several pages of disclaimers (this is an art, not a science), and the appraiser's qualifications.

**Appraised value**  Market value; an opinion of an appraiser, which is based upon an interpretation of facts and judgments and their processing into an estimate of value, as of a stated date. While the term "appraised value" is generic, for our purposes its specific meaning is the market value, obtained by direct comparison of similar, recent house sales.

**Appraiser office**  (or assessor office or department)  The county department charged with valuing the property in the county for tax purposes. In small counties, there may be only one appraiser in the office. In large counties, he may have hundreds of assistants.

**Appreciation**  Increase in value because of inflation, increased cost to reproduce a similar building on a similar site, greater demand, improved economic conditions, improved transportation, or community growth.

**Appurtenance**  Something that has been added or attached (with screws, bolts, pipes, and so forth) to a property, which becomes a part of the property and is sold with it. A chandelier or a picture screwed into the wall are appurtenances, but a lamp or a picture hanging on a wall nail are not appurtenances.

**Arithmetic mean**  Synonym for "average"; quotient of a sum of values divided by the number of values. (For example, the mean of 3, 6, and 12 is 21 divided by 3, or 7). Disadvantage is that the mean is distorted by extreme figures.

**Arm's length**  A sale in the open market, unaffected by abnormal pressure on buyer or seller, involving normal competitive negotiation, buyer and seller being reasonably informed. A related-parties sale is *not* an arm's length sale. (For example, a father may sell his house to his son for $20,000, when the market is $100,000.)

**Array**  The listing of a set of observations, usually from low to high, or large to small.

**Assessment**
1. The value assigned to the property for ad valorem tax purposes; the county appraiser's appraised value.
2. A single charge levied against a parcel of real estate to pay for a public improvement, such as curbs, fire hydrants, or sewers. Often called a "special assessment."
3. An official determination of the amount of money a parcel owner must pay to defray the cost of a public improvement.
4. **Eminent domain assessment**—Official determination of the amount the

government will pay to take all or part of a parcel, for a school, road widening, or other public improvement.

**Assessment base** The total assessed value of all property within a designated area, such as a tax district or city. Synonym: property tax base.

**Assessment district** Jurisdiction in which the special assessment is made, such as neighborhood, city, county, or state.

**Assessment period** (or cycle or frequency) Period during which all property in the jurisdiction must be assessed or reassessed. Often, cycle is five years.

**Assessment sales ratio** (or coefficient of dispersion) Assessed value divided by sales price. A neighborhood with an assessment ratio of 0.9 indicates a $100,000 house should have an assessed value of $90,000.

**Assessor** One who assesses property for ad valorem taxes.

**Auction** An advertised sale where many potential buyers vie for the property in a formal setting, with an auctioneer presiding and governing the process. In an *absolute* auction the property is sold to the highest bidder regardless of price; in a *relative* auction the property is sold to the highest bidder subject to confirmation by owner.

**Basis** The portion of the property value that is likely to be affected by depreciation or capital improvement. Usually, the purchase price.

**Basis point** One hundredth of one percentage point, or .0001; refers to mortgages.

**Bench mark** U.S. Geological Survey and other permanently fixed markers in the ground indicating elevation, geographical points, used as starting points by surveyors. Generically, a "starting point," a standard or base from which estimates are made. See p. 11 remarks about U.S. Geological Survey.

**Bi-level** A split-level house.

**Blight** Decay, in a neighborhood, caused by declining homeowner pride or declining public services; also applied to plants, as palm tree (lethal yellowing) blight, or Dutch elm blight.

**Block** In legal parcel identification, the second smallest unit of description, as "township 50, range 42, section 6, subdivision 89, Block 5, lot 13." (See Figure 2-2.)

**Blockbusting** Buying property at depressed prices in a changing neighborhood. Usually a family of another class or race is introduced into the area. Then unscrupulous buyers appear to buy property at low prices and subsequently resell the same property to newcomers at inflated prices.

**Board of equalization** (BofE—or board of appeals, property adjustment appeals board, board of assessment)  A quasi-judicial assembly of tax- and real-estate-oriented professionals designed to value, or assess, all property uniformly. Property owners obtain assessment reductions when they can show that their assessments are higher than the assessment process would indicate.

**Book value**  The capital amount shown on the account books. Usually, it equals the original cost minus reserves for depreciation plus capital additions.

**Brick veneer**  A non-load-bearing brick facade.

**Buffer strip**  A parcel of land separating differently zoned areas, frequently landscaped for screening. It is designed to prohibit incompatible abutting areas.

**Building capitalization rate**  The return *on* plus the return *of* capital invested in improvements, separate and apart from capital invested in the land. It is used in residual techniques that separate property income into land and improvements (building) income components.

**Building residual technique**  The technique of estimating the contribution of improvements to the present worth or value of the entire property, over and above the site value. Similar to allocation, or abstraction.

1. Deduct return attributable to the land (independent of building) from net operating income.
2. Capitalize the residual income that is the return to the building (including recapture) to get building value.

**Bulkhead**  A retaining wall erected along the waterline that separates the land from the water. Often the top of the bulkhead wall is several feet above the water.

**Bundle of rights theory**  Real estate ownership may embrace many rights, such as the rights to sell, bequeath, or transfer; underground (mineral) rights; and sky rights.

**Cantilever**  Overhang, as a tier of high-rise-condo patio floors that extend or project beyond the load-bearing structure.

**Cape Cod house**  Typically, a one-and-a-half story, white frame, dormered second-story windowed house.

**Capital expenditures** (or expenses)  Improvements on land. Includes building, new roof, new A/C, termite inspection or extermination. Opposite is *fixed expense.*

**Capital gain**  Net value minus book value (adjusted cost). Used in income tax preparation.

**Capital recovery** (recapture)  Return *of* investment, as distinguished from return *on* investment, usually expressed as an annual rate. It is applied to wasting assets, which have a finite economic life. Synonymous with amortization rate, to express investor goal of recovering his equity investment over a specified period of time.

**Capitalization**
1. Converting a future income stream into a present value, or present worth. In real estate, capitalization is called *discounting.*
2. Accountants use the word as an addition to capital, in appraisal terms.

**Capitalization rate** (or overall rate)  For our purposes, the net operating income divided by the value, or sales price.

**Capitalize**  To convert future values into current value, or present worth.

**Carport**  An open-sided, roofed (not awninged) car shelter. A carport is not counted in adjustable square feet.

**Cash equivalent**  The cash value, rather than the note value. You would be ahead if you could buy a loaf of bread for a $1 million note (mortgage) at 20 percent interest, with all principal and interest due in 100 years! Also a sometime synonym for fair market value.

**Cash flow**  The flow of cash in and out of a house or investment. For real estate, see *net operating income.*

**Certiorari**  A writ from a superior to an inferior court officer, board, or tribunal, directing that a document be sent up for review. A remedy for judicial review. In Florida, tax appeal board hearing results do not bear on circuit court petitions.

**Change, principle of**  Appraisal concept. Cause and effect, supply and demand result in constant upward and downward movement of building values over time.

**Chief hearing officer**  Special master, board of equalization chairman.

**Circuit breaker**  Tax relief usually limited to elderly or poor residential property owners. Tax liability is limited to a percentage of owner's income.

**Civil law**  Noncriminal law. Usually, torts (injuries) to the corporate or individual person. Usually involves money as compensation. Includes constitutional and Bill of Rights law. Real estate is governed by civil law.

**Cloud on title**   An encumbrance that may affect property ownership and right to transfer (sell).

**Coastal Construction Control Line** (or CCCL)   If your property is on a lake or on the sea, check with your state department of natural resources or county planning department. On the Gulf, East, and West coasts, and on the Great Lakes, this may apply to you now. New construction seaward of the CCCL is henceforth (check the date) restricted to tennis courts, pool, and **frisable** construction. Frisable construction is more able to withstand gale-force winds and flood waters than traditional construction, and it is less likely to damage neighboring properties if blown or floated away.

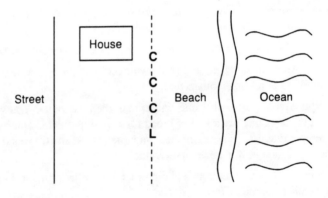

**Coefficient of Dispersion** (or CD)   A U.S. Census Bureau ratio that compares the assessed value of properties with sales prices. Ideally, the sales prices should be 10 percent above the assessment values, when the assessment is supposed to be 100 percent of the value. Ten percent of the sales price is marketing expense (broker's commission, attorney's fees, and so forth). (See the discussion of the CD in Chapter 2.)

The 1990 census data, along with the CD, may not be available yet. But you can develop your own area CD, **before you do your lowball appraisal.** Take 30 recent house sales near you and run a CD on them. You can get the sales prices and assessments from a realtor or the tax roll. This will give you the overall picture. But remember, your house may still be overassessed because of some unique qualities, such as a leaky roof, a busy traffic corner, or a recent fire in the kitchen.

**Common wall**   One wall separating two residences, as in condos and townhouses.

**Concurrency**   All infrastructure has to be in place or provided for, before start of construction, so as to support the proposed development. Infrastructure can include all major and minor roads, storm and drain sewers, schools, fire and police stations, parks, and other specified amenities and zoning.

**Condominium**   Individual fee ownership of whole units or separate portions (percentages) of multiunit buildings, and joint ownership of common areas, such as the pool and lawn. Not a *"cooperative."*

**Constructive notice**   Notice via public records. Law presumes everyone has the same knowledge of all documents properly recorded as if actually acquainted with them.

**Cooperative**   Individual units owned via stock in corporation. Person has right to live in a particular unit, pays a percentage of expenses and taxes, and has transfer rights.

**Cost approach**   One of the three basic appraisal approaches. Principle is that the informed purchaser would pay no more than the cost of producing a substitute property with the same utility as the subject property. It is especially apropos when the subject has unique or new improvements that have no market peers.

**County**   The largest division of local government in all states except Alaska (borough) and Louisiana (parish).

**Curable depreciation**   Physical deterioration (such as roof leaks) and functional obsolescence (4 bed/1 bath) that is economically feasible to cure (repair). A prudent homeowner will do so. The estimate of this depreciation is usually equal to the cost of the repairs.

**Date of appraisal**   The date on the appraisal to which the value estimate applies. Often it is the inspection date, as this date protects the appraiser against subsequent property value changes.

**Debt**   Money that has been borrowed for a specific period. Debt may be either secured or unsecured.

**Debt financing**   Paying for a property with partial or full borrowed funds. The real estate itself serves as security, or collateral, for the debt.

**Debt service**   The periodic (usually monthly) payment that retires the loan (principal) and pays the cost of borrowing (interest).

**Deed**   A legal instrument, in writing, which, when executed and delivered, conveys an estate or interest in real property. There are different kinds of deeds: administrator's deed, bond for deed, committee deed, executor's deed, mortgage deed, quitclaim deed, trust deed, warranty deed.

**Default**   The failure to fulfill a contractual agreement.

**Density zoning**   A system of zoning or land use controls under which residential occupancy is limited by the number of families per unit of land area in one plot, such as an acre, rather than by limiting the number of families permitted to dwell in one structure.

**Depreciation**   Loss of value, or utility, for any reason. The result of deterioration or obsolescence, evidenced by wear and tear, decay, rot, leaks, cracks, or other structural defects. Obsolescence is divided into (1) functional obsolescence (poor floor plan, oversized, aged), and (2) economic obsolescence (rising crime, traffic, disharmony, new high school or prison). Depreciation is also the actual decline in market value of the improvement (building and appurtenances) between the time of purchase and the time of sale.

**Diminishing utility**   The effect of wear and tear; a house wears out (roof, plumbing and wiring, and so forth). The consumption of each succeeding unit yields less satisfaction than the preceding unit.

**Direct capitalization**   The conversion of anticipated (future) net income into present value by dividing the income by an appropriate rate, which reflects the prevailing relationship of net income to selling price for comparable properties being sold on the open market. Direct capitalization for land was the discount rate, while direct capitalization for land and improvements utilizes the overall rate, or the net operating income divided by the sale price.

**Direct sales comparison approach** (also called market approach, or market data approach)   The main residential appraisal analysis approach. This approach's main premise is that an informed buyer pays no more than a comparable property would sell for. He or she compares existing similar properties with the same utilities and in the same price range and makes a choice. This approach is applicable when the area's verifiable sales volume is sufficient to find good comparables. Conversely, in an inactive market, or where there are no good comparables, the direct sales comparison approach is relatively unreliable.

**Discounted cash flow**   Present worth of future income stream, or of future cash benefits, usually involving equity investment.

**Discounted cash flow method**   A way of differentiating cash flow variables by discounting the cash flows to their present values. Two discounted cash flow methods are IRR (internal rate of return) and NPV (net present value).

**Discounted rate of return**  Synonym for internal rate of return.

**Discounting**  A time-value-of-money concept holding that future income benefits are worth less than the same income or benefits now. Such benefits decrease in value as their receipt goes farther out into the future. In appraisal analysis, discounting is applying a specific rate derived from the market to the anticipated future income stream to develop a present worth estimate.

For example, you own a mortgage paying you $500 per month at 10 percent interest for 10 years, and your mortgage broker has a buyer who wants to get a 15 percent return for his investment. The mortgage's present (discounted return *of* investment) value is $38,255 without the buyer's 15 percent return. With his 15 percent return (*on* investment) the discounted value is $30,991. Note that his 15 percent return in present dollars is $38,255 minus $30991, or $7,264. Also note that the total dollars received **over the 10-year period** would be $500 per month times 12 months, times 10 years, or $60,000.

**Disincentive** (or "Why work?" threshold)  Point at which wages less taxes make not working more attractive than working. Often characterized by worker ennui, "laziness," rebelliousness, strikes, emigration. All government taxes in the United States today average 34 percent of American income. The threshold varies according to the type of work and amount of compensation of the worker. This is a theme of Reaganomics economist Arthur Laffer.

**District**  A unit of government that has the authority to levy taxes and issue bonds to finance schools.

**Dormer**  A window projecting from a pitched roof, often seen in one-and-a-half-floor Cape Cod houses. The projecting window has its own pitched roof.

**Drainfield**  An area containing a system of underground lateral pipes designed to remove water, sewage, or other types of liquid overflow.

**Dry rot**  A decay of seasoned wood caused by fungus.

**Drywall** (sheetrock).   Usually gypsum board, about one-half inch by four inches by six inches. Sometimes refers to plywood or fiberboard.

**Dutch door**  A door divided horizontally in the middle so that the bottom half can remain closed while the top half remains open.

**Easement**   As in utility or street easements, often called public easements. That interest held by the street authority or utility company enabling the utility to use the strip of land for water, gas, sewer, and electric purposes. It restricts but does not abridge fee owner rights. Easements are of three kinds: overhead, surface, and subsurface.

**Eave**   the lower or outer edge of a roof projecting over the side walls of a structure.

**Economic** (or physical age)   The assigned lifespan of the house (usually 40 to 50 years) less estimated deterioration, usually expressed as "remaining life." If an appraiser's inspection indicates a 40-year-old house with a 50-year life has just been completely remodeled, he may assign a "30-year remaining life" to that structure.

**Economic or external obsolescence**   Reduction in desirability or useful life as a result of economic, environmental, or external forces that reduce demand in the market area. Is distinct from physical and functional obsolescence.

**Effective age**   If an area's average house life is 50 years, and the subject house is 10 years old, its chronological life is 10 years. If it is well maintained, its effective age may only be 6 years. Or, conversely, if it was rented to male college students at a nearby school, its effective life may be 15 years.

**Effective gross income**   The potential gross income less the vacancy and bad debt rate.

**Effluent**   Liquid sewage after having been partially or completely purified.

**Elevation**   Also called altitude. Height above sea level, usually expressed in feet.

**Environmental deficiency**   Factors promoting blight and deterioration. Examples are overcrowding, inadequate utilities, obsolescent building (loose asbestos), and underground soil contamination. In some parts of Florida with many septic tanks, the water table is only three or four feet below ground level. During heavy rains, the water table rises, carrying contagious septic tank bacteria and viruses to the surface. Children playing in this water after heavy rains contract meningitis.

**Equity ratio**   The ratio of down payment to total price. The debt-free part or fraction of an investment.

**Erosion**   The loss of topsoil or surface land due to the action of wind and water. The Grand Canyon is an extreme example of erosion over millions of years.

**Escrow**   A reserve account, or a savings account, put aside for a special reason. For example, the lender (your mortgage company) puts aside about one-twelfth of your estimated November (or whenever) tax bill. When your bill arrives at the mortgage company, it is paid immediately. You get your 4 percent discount. But rarely is your assessment appealed because the mortgage company is not organized to appeal taxes.

**Estate**   A right or interest in property. Property, including stocks and securities, of a deceased person.

**Estimate**   An appraiser's opinion of the value of a property.

**Exclusive agency listing**   A real estate broker acquires the right to represent the owner in the sale of the property. The exclusive agent may sell the house himself, in which case he obtains the whole commission, or he may sell through another agent, in which case he gets half the commission.

**Expropriation**   In Canada and Great Britain, synonym for eminent domain.

**FDIC** (Federal Deposit Insurance Corporation)   The government corporation that insures bank deposits (and since the FSLIC demise, S&L deposits). Most RTC executives are former or present FDIC employees.

**Fee simple**   Absolute; without limitations as to heirs, but subject to eminent domain, escheat, police power, and taxation.

**FHA** (Federal Housing Administration)   Part of Housing and Urban Development Department, whose director is a member of the president's cabinet.

**FHLMC** (Federal Home Loan Mortgage Corporation, or Freddie Mac)   Like FNMA. Primarily buys multifamily units, such as condos, apartments.

**Final value estimate**   The appraiser's opinion of the value of the property after considering and reconciling the sales approach (primary) with the cost (and sometimes) the income approach.

**Fire retardant**   Material that resists heat and resultant combustion.

**Fixed assets**   Property not easily convertible to cash, such as real estate, as contrasted with stocks and bonds, which are liquid (instantly convertible).

**Fixed homeowner expenses**   Expenses that do not vary, such as ad valorem taxes and insurance. Actually, they tend to rise a bit each year. Opposite is capital expenses.

**Flat roof**  Roof pitch sufficient for drainage, does not exceed 20 degrees.

**Floor-area ratio**  Total square feet of a building (house, all floors) divided by the lot (site) area. For example, a 2,500-square-foot floor area building on a 10,000-square-foot lot has a floor-area ratio of .25.

**FNMA** (Federal National Mortgage Association, or Fannie Mae)  Buys mortgages from lending institutions such as banks and savings and loans, and packages many mortgages into multi–million dollar packages, selling them to large investors. A quasi-independent government corporation. It authored the residential appraisal forms now in use throughout the United States, and monitors residential appraisal practices, adjusting the forms as it deems necessary. Primarily buys single-family home mortgages.

**Folio number** (or property, or parcel ID number—PIN or PID)  The property parcel's unique ID, similar to one's Social Security number.

**Foreclosure**  The legal process by which a mortgagee, when the mortgagor defaults on the loan, forces property sale to recover his lost payments.

**Front elevation**  The front view of a building.

**Front foot**  The number of streetside linear feet, assuming house faces street. Often parcels are valued in terms of front feet.

**Functional curable obsolescence**  A 4 bed/1 bath house appraisal comes in at $90,000. Adding a second bath costs $5,000, and raises the house value $5,500, to $95,500. The $500 increase in value makes this obsolescence **functionally curable.**

**Functional incurable obsolescence**  In the above example, the second bath raises the value only $4,500, to $94,500. Adding the second bath would not pay for itself in the sale of the house.

**Functional obsolescence**  A structure fails to adequately perform its function; 4 bed/1 bath for five people; kitchen too small; have to go through bedroom to get to kitchen; and so forth.

**Functional utility value**  Measure of usefulness, re traffic patterns, current market tastes, ceiling heights, and so forth, expressed in monetary terms.

**Gable**  The end of a building, usually triangular.

**Garden apartments**  Two- or three-story walk-up apartments in a well-landscaped setting.

**Government lots**   Land areas that could not be divided into sections and quarters under government survey.

**Grade**   Slope of a surface. A 10 percent grade means 10 foot elevation rise for every 100 feet of horizontal surface.

**Gradient**   The degree of inclination of (usually) a road, or (occasionally) a fill.

**Gross income (rent) multiplier**   Sales price divided by potential gross income or effective gross income (either one or the other—not interchangeable). Example: sales price of $960,000, potential gross income of $12,000; the GIM is 960 divided by 12, or 80: 80 times $12,000 yields $960,000.

**Grout**   A thin fluid mortar used between tiles in bathrooms and between small masonry joints.

**Gunite**   A cementlike mixture sprayed from a nozzle under air compression.

**Gypsum**   Hydrated (watered) calcium sulphate. Ingredient of plaster of paris. Gypsum boards are also called sheetrock (wallboards), a substitute for plaster.

**Header**   In carpentry, a wood beam set in the wall at a 90 degree angle to provide support for the floor, and so forth. In computing, the top of the page ID.

**Heat pump**   A reverse-cycle refrigeration unit that can be used for heating or cooling.

**Height density**   Zoning regulation to control building height and thus population.

**Heterogeneous**   In real estate, a diverse group of property uses in one area, or a polyethnic or polyglottal grouping of different ethnic or racial groups in one area. Los Angeles is ethnically heterogeneous; Houston is heterogeneous realty-wise.

**Highest and best use**   The most profitable use of the parcel. Qualifications: legal; most reasonably probable; physically possible; financially feasible. Maximizes return to property owners.

**Homestead**   Fixed residence or dwelling of the head of a family. Includes land and improvements.

**Homestead exemption**   A release from a part of the property tax levy; exclusion of property from legal action from creditors; exclusion from forced sale.

**Homogeneous** In real estate, area having similar property types or ethnic or cultural groups.

**Hydraulic cement** Cement that hardens under water. Used for bridge bulwarking and so forth.

**I beam** A steel beam used for building support, and resembling the letter I.

**Impact costs** The costs associated with an improvement infrastructure.

**Improved land** Land that has been improved with landscaping or buildings.

**Improved property** (Improvements) The real estate other than the land; the building and property attached to the building.

**Improvements**
1. *Improvements on land*—buildings, fences, retaining walls, driveways.
2. *Improvements to land*—Usually, to make property usable: curbs, sidewalks, lighting, sewers, drains, fill.

**Income approach to value** Only used in commercial property, but this includes rental residential units. This converts a future income stream (the rent) into a value estimate. The income stream is discounted to get its present value. On the URAR-1004, the income approach asks for the gross rent multiplier (GRM) to obtain value. For example, $1,000 per month rent times 110 GRM equals $110,000 value for the unit. A more professional method, used for commercial properties, divides the net operating income (NOI) by the sale price (or the value indicated by the assessed value) to yield the overall capitalization rate. For example, an $8,000 NOI on a property valued at $66,667 equals a 12 percent capitalization rate; the formula is NOI/Value = Cap Rate; I/V = R. Therefore I/R = V, or $8,000/.12 = $66,667 value.

**Income multiplier** A factor that is the reciprocal of the overall rate. In the above (*income approach to value*) example, it is $66,667/$8,000 = 8.83; income multiplier = sale price or value/net operating income.

**Incurable depreciation** A physical deterioration that cannot be fixed, such as a poor house layout, or a deterioration that, if fixed for $3,000, would not add $3,000 to the market value of the house.

**Indirect cost** Not included in direct construction or land acquisition costs. Examples are fees, financing costs, insurance and taxes during construction, title, surveys, and interest on land.

**Inflation** A relatively sudden large increase in the cost of goods and services. "Creeping inflation" is an almost unnoticeable gradual increase of, for example, 5 percent per year. Inflation is a highly mortgaged home-owner's friend. A 1978, $100,000 house with a $90,000 fixed (frozen interest rate) mortgage was worth about $135,000 in 1980. The home-owner only put $10,000 into the down payment, so his two-year return *on* (not *of*) his investment of $10,000 was $35,000, or 350 percent, in the 1978–80 period. Not bad. But this is an exceptional example of 15 percent to 20 percent inflation. In the last few years of "creeping inflation" (about 5 percent), many residential areas in the Oilpatch and even California have **decreased** in value.

**Infrastructure**   Roads, water and sewer, parks, interstate and express-way ingress or egress, police and fire, height, air, pollution and similar items that must be addressed, analyzed, and dealt with before breaking ground for a proposed development.

**Insulation**   Material used to reduce the transfer of heat, cold, or sound. It is also the nonconductive covering of electric wires.

**Insurance**   The business of insuring property against fire and certain other specified contingencies, such as theft or flood.

**Interest**   Money earned by the use of capital, also called principal. Return *on* principal is distinguished from return *of* principal. In a mortgage, in-terest is the return *on* the principal. Interest could be said to be the "rent" for the use of capital.

**Interest rate**   Rate of return *on* an investment, not return *of* investment.

**Interior trim**   Interior finish, such as baseboard, molding, and casing.

**Internal rate of return**   A common measure of real (income) property value. It is the rate that discounts all returns to equal the original invest-ment.

**Intestate**   Dying without a will.

**Inverse condemnation**   Example: After your house in the woods is built in accordance with zoning and permits, the U.S. Corps of Engineers orders you to restore the area to its original condition. After completing the restoration, the U.S. government reimburses you for your expenses.

**Invoice**   A bill.

**Invoice window**   Small squares on the invoice that are dedicated to spe-cialized functions, such as the amount of money in mortgagor's tax ac-count.

**Jack rafter, jack stud**    An auxiliary, supporting piece of lumber, "jerry-built."

**Jalousies**    Adjustable glass louvers in windows and sometimes doors that regulate light and air.

**Junction box**    Where the small electrical circuits join the main one; also called circuit box.

**Laminated wood**    The fibers, or wood grain, of the various glued-together plies run parallel. Assembled crosswise, the plies are collectively called plywood.

**Land residual technique**    A valuation method in which the income is split between the land and the improvements (buildings), and then the land income is capitalized into value. Usually, the building is valued independently from the land. The annual return on the building value (return *on* investment and provision for return *of* investment) is deducted from the property's anticipated net operating income (NOI of land and building). The residual amount, attributable to land, is capitalized at the germane risk (discount) rate to indicate land value. For new houses, the value assigned to the improvements is cost, which assumes no accrued depreciation, and also construction at proper current cost, or the depreciated value at the time of the appraisal.

An old house is hypothesized as a new one, with subsequent building costs, as a basis for estimating the net income attributable to the land.

**Landscaping**    Adding trees, shrubs, hillocks, rocks, and sod to a site, as a beautiful backdrop, or frame, for the house.

**Lateral**    Extensions of a main line, such as water or sewer lines, or a septic tank.

**Leachate**    A liquid discharge seeping into the ground from a hazardous or potentially harmful waste material, such as paint, heavy metals, or petroleum products (which form carcinogenic hydrocarbons).

**Leader**    A downspout carrying rainwater from the roof gutters to the ground.

**Lease**    A written rental agreement between tenant and owner/landlord or landlord's agent.

**Lessee**    A tenant.

**Lessor**    A landlord.

**Lien**    A charge against the property in which the property is made security for the payment of a debt.

**Life**   The anticipated physical or economic usefulness of an improvement (land has no life, as it is assumed to be indestructible). For appraisal purposes, a house's life is assumed to be 50 to 70 years. For mortgage purposes, the building life has to be at least as long as the term of the mortgage.

**Linkages**   Time and space relationship between a house and supporting facilities, such as schools or shopping and employment facilities. Linkages affect a house's value.

**Lintel**   A wood, stone, or metal length placed above a window or door to support the wall immediately above the opening.

**Liquid assets**   Assets immediately convertible into cash. Houses are not liquid assets, because of the length of time necessary to liquidate them.

**Liquidation price**   A "quick sale" price, usually considerably below the market.

**Lis pendens**   Notice of a suit pending.

**Listing contract**   A written agreement between the property owner and a real estate broker, employing the broker to sell the owner's real estate.

**Littoral rights**   The rights of an owner of a parcel bordering on a body of water to enjoy those rights. Not riparian rights.

**Load-bearing wall**   A wall that supports the structure(s) (roof, upper wall) above it.

**Loan-to-value ratio**   The ratio of the mortgage loan to the value of the property, expressed as a percentage. A mortgage with an 80 percent loan-to-value ratio means that the property owner has 20 percent equity in the house. After five years, however, the property may have appreciated to the point that the loan-to-value ratio is 70 percent (that is, the property is worth about 10 percent more than when purchased).

**Locational** (Extrinsic, Environmental, or Economic) **Obsolescence**   Loss of property value as a result of nearby outside forces, such as a new prison or a hazardous waste dump.

**Lot**   A subdivision is divided into blocks (Block 1, Block 2, and so forth). Each block is divided into lots. One block may have 5 lots, another 50 lots.

**Lot and block**   The smallest part of a legal description of a property parcel. Several or more lots form a block; several or more blocks compose a subdivision. Several or more subdivisions or unused land form a section (one square mile).

**Louver**  Slots or fins over an opening, such as glass strips over a window, or fluorescent light filters, or a building or garden sunshade.

**Maintenance**  The process of keeping a property "up to snuff," to preserve its value.

**Manufactured housing**  A house whose walls, wiring, plumbing, ceiling, and exterior, including roof, are made in a factory and shipped to a site with a prepared foundation. Also called a modular house. Usually as durable as conventionally built home. Not a mobile home.

**Market data approach** (also called sales approach, comparable sales approach, market approach)  The principal appraisal technique for determining a residential property value. Three or more properties, similar to the subject, are compared to the subject in order to estimate the subject value.

**Market value**  The highest price a property will bring in a fair and open market, with a prudent and typically motivated and knowledgeable buyer and seller. The following elements are present: (1) subject is on market for a reasonable time; (2) payment is cash or equivalent; (3) average (by community standards) financing. State supreme courts define market value in slightly different ways, and these definitions are subject to frequent change. Appraisers should find out the exact definition of market value in their state.

**Marshall & Swift Valuation Service**  One of the authoritative guides for estimating the cost of building a structure, using both the component (4/cubic foot of concrete, of roofing, and so forth) and the cost per square foot of air-conditioned and non–air-conditioned (garage, porch) space, landscaping, and so forth. One of the "MVS" specialties is residential structures. Dodge Building Services and others also have roughly similar services, used by architects, engineers, appraisers, and allied field personnel.

**Masonry**  Stone, brick, tile, cement, or similar building material.

**Mass appraising**  Appraising many properties at one time by using standard techniques, such as multivariate analysis, or linear regression, prototype ("typical") properties, and other appraisal techniques with a view toward achieving equalization of properties' taxes—that is, "fair" property taxation.

**Master plan** (also called city plan, general plan)  The overall, long-range official government plan to develop or redevelop an area. Some components of such a plan are land use, thoroughfares, community facilities, and public improvements. Knowledge of a master plan can be instrumental in obtaining tax relief, for example, in the case of a property owner whose house is next to a proposed high-voltage transmission line.

**Mean** A measure of central tendency. Generically, the "average," or the sum of the integers divided by the number of integers (2 + 3 + 4 + 11 = 20; 20/5 = 4 = Mean). (See *mode, median, standard deviation.*)

**Median** The middle number in a progressive series (in the series 1, 2, 3, 4, 8, 11, 56, 4 is the median, or middle, number).

**Metes and bounds** A description of a land parcel using angles east or west of due north and south and distances in feet or chains (a chain is 66 feet), and such as U.S. Geodetic Survey and subsidiary benchmarks. Example: From SW cor POB (Point of Beginning) 330' (Ft) E (east), 90 degrees N 660', 90 deg W 330', 90 deg S 660' to POB.

**Millage** A mill is $.001, or one-tenth of a cent; 26 miles is $.026, or 2.6 cents. Tax millage is expressed in mills per thousand dollars of assessed property. Thus a lot tax assessed at $1,000 value, at a 26 mill rate, owes $1,000 times $.026, or $26, in taxes.

**Mobile Home** Sometimes erroneously called manufactured housing. Usually 8 to 16 feet wide and 20 to 40 feet long, and originally, at least, on wheels. Less durable than manufactured or prefabricated homes. Also called trailer housing.

**Mode** the most frequently occurring value in an array of numbers (in the sequence 6, 4, 9, 7, 5, 6, 3, 3, 6, 8, 6 is the mode number, appearing three times).

**Most probable sales price** Elements: (1) exposed to the market for a reasonable time; (2) under market conditions prevailing at the time of the appraisal.

**Multiple variable regression analysis** Measuring the simultaneous influence of many dependent variables upon one independent variable. In our case the independent variable is a house's market value. A few of the many dependent variables are time, bedrooms and baths, living square footage, distance from subject, and age of house. When perfected, regression will predict the sale price within 5 percent. However, many are not certain it can be perfected, for single house values, because there are too many independent variables (as yet unquantifiable factors to consider). It is probably just a matter of time before it becomes more widely employed in county assessors' mass appraisal work.

**Neighborhood**    A portion of a larger community having rather homogeneous characteristics, such as type of buildings, business enterprises, or socioeconomic groups. Often defined by specific boundaries, such as an expressway or a park. The legal "subdivision" may or may not conform to the boundaries of the neighborhood.

**Neighborhood life cycle**    Generality (not always true) that a residential area is born (roads and utilities installed), grows (houses built), matures (period after no vacant lots remain), declines (as houses age, utilities services or homeowner pride and upkeep decline, crime rises), and death (South Bronx burned-out areas) or rebirth (Baltimore waterfront).

**Net income multiplier**    The number derived by dividing the sale price or value by the net operating income (NOI). Sale price of $90,000 divided by an NOI of $9,000 equals a net income multiplier of 10. Similar to price/earnings ratio. It is the reciprocal of overall rate. Used on rental houses only.

**Net income ratio**    Net income divided by effective gross income. The part of gross income remaining after all expenses except depreciation and debt service are deducted.

**Net lease**    In addition to the rent, the lessee (tenant) pays all property charges, such as taxes, insurance, maintenance, and assessments. "Net net and net net net" are redundant synonyms of net lease (rentals only).

**Net operating income** (NOI; symbol is I)    One of the more important concepts in income (rental) property. I equals R times V, where R is overall rate and V is sale price or value.

| | | |
|---|---|---|
| Gross potential income | $ 100,000 | (as if fully rented) |
| Vacancy and bad debt at 5 percent | − (5,000) | |
| Effective gross income | = 95,000 | |
| Operating expenses at 40 percent | −(38,000) | |
| **Net operating income** | = 57,000 | |
| Debt service (mortgages) | −(35,000) | |
| Cash throw off | = 22,000 | |
| Taxes (includes depreciation) | − (8,000) | |
| After-tax cash flow **net income** | = 16,000 | |

**Net present value (NPV)**    The difference between the cost of an investment and the discounted present value of the investment's future income stream. When the NPV is positive, the proposal is good; when it is zero, investment is marginal; when NPV is negative, the proposal is not good.

**Net worth**   Assets less liabilities. Equity. Assets of $100 less $30 of liabilities equals $70 net worth.

**NIBD**   Net income before depreciation.

**Nogging**   Brick fill in a frame wall, or wood placed in a masonry wall to receive nails.

**Nonconforming building**   A building not conforming to a zoning ordinance, for example, a duplex or retail store in a single-family-zoned area.

**Obsolescence**   A cause of depreciation. Loss of desirability brought on by new inventions and designs, improved production processes, or other factors. There are two kinds of obsolescence: (1) economic (also called environmental, external, or locational); and (2) functional. (See *depreciation.*)

**Operating expenses**   Difference between effective gross income and NOI.

**Overage income**   Rental income over and above a guaranteed minimum rental sum, usually based upon store's volume. Example: $1,000 per month rent plus 1 percent of gross in excess of $100,000 per month. If the lessee did $150,000 one month, his rent would be $1,500.

**Overall rate**   Net operating income (NOI)/sale price or value. R = I/V. Includes return *of* and *on* investment.

**Overimprovement**   Most expensive house on the block; $20,000 pool in $8,000 pool neighborhood (pool **might** add $7,000 to $9,000 to parcel value).

**Parameter**   A single characteristic or variable of a population that may vary over a range of values when taken individually. A boundary.

**Parapet**   A wall erected along the edge of a cliff, bridge terrace, or roof, for protection or water control.

**Parcel**   The parcel may only have one lot. It may have several, even 20, lots. Or the parcel may not be divided into lots. It may be divided into tracts. The parcel may have one or several tracts. Tracts are abbreviated Tr on plats, which are maps of subdivisions.

**Parquet floor**   Prefinished, thin square or rectangular wooden blocks.

**Party wall**   Common wall serving two property owners, as a rowhouse wall.

**Patio**   Open, **nonroofed** area, paved, usually abutting a house. Not a porch.

**Penthouse**   An apartment or house on the top floor or roof of a multistory building.

**Personal property**   Generally, movable items, such as furniture and equipment that is not screwed, bolted, or otherwise permanently attached to the building. Nonfixtures.

**Physical assets**   Land, building, machinery, equipment, and so forth.

**Physical curable deterioration**   Deterioration the prudent buyer would correct after buying the property. The cost of the correction would be no more than the projected financial appreciation of the property. Sometimes called "deferred maintenance," or rehabilitation.

**Physical deterioration**   Reduction in value or utility due to impairment. Usually divided into curable and incurable.

**Physical incurable deterioration**   Cost to fix exceeds the projected financial appreciation. In appraisal analysis, it is divided into short (everything but the house's exterior walls) and long (exterior walls only). Roof is short-lived.

**Picture window**   Large window, sometimes consisting of panes, sometimes of one large fixed plate-glass sheet, providing much light and a view.

**Pile**   A wooden or steel-encased concrete column driven into the ground to support a building or other structure.

**Pitch**   The slope of a roof, usually expressed in inches of rise per linear foot.

**Plan**   Blueprints. Horizontal and vertical drawings of a house, in cross section, floor by floor.

**Planned unit development** (or PUD)   Commercial, industrial, or residential. Higher density than non-PUDs in most residential cases, but with green belts and even large parklike areas.

**Plat**   A map or sketch of a geographical area showing the boundaries of the properties. Often shows lot, block, subdivision, section, range, and township numbers or perimeters. Sometimes used as synonym for survey, which is a plat of an individual lot or parcel.

**Plottage**   Process of adding (usually small) land increments to a parcel for the purpose of increasing overall value.

**Plume**   The underground "island" of leachate. It is formed by the hydrological (water) underground flow. Usually measured in cubic yards.

**Plywood**   An odd number of layers of wood veneer glued together with the grain at right angles.

**Point**   One percentage of a mortgage. A $100,000 mortgage for 29 years at 11 percent interest with 3 points means that the purchaser will pay $3,000 to get the mortgage. This same mortgage at 9 percent interest will have more points, perhaps as many as 10. Why? Because the monthly payments will be less . . . so you pay more up front.

**Prehearing conference**   Meeting with the county appraiser/assessor or his or her representative before filing a tax assessment reduction appeal.

**Present value** (PV)   Current monetary value, or discounted value of a future income stream. Sometimes used incorrectly as synonym for present worth.

**Present worth** (of future income stream)   Present value of collections at a specified future date(s), discounted from those times to the present date at a specified rate of discount.

**Principal**   A capital sum of money invested in a project. The amount of money the bank lends the house buyer, or mortgagor, excluding points and other charges. Not the interest.

**Probability**   The number between 0 and 1 that represents the likelihood of an event occurring. A 0.3 or 30 percent chance of rain means that there are 3 chances in 10 of rain falling.

**Profit and loss statement**   A prepared document from the books and records of a landlord, indicating all of the rented house's rental income and expenses, usually for one year, indicating the end of year profit or loss. Required for rental house appeal.

**Property**   For our purposes, land and building combined.

**Property legal description**   Unequivocal identification of the property, not the folio/PIN/PID. Example: Lot 4, Block 15, Happy Acres, PB (Plat Book/page) 124/67.

**Property line**   The boundary between two properties, or between a property and the street.

**Purchase money mortgage** (PMM)   The seller lends money to the buyer by means of a note, or mortgage, which is usually subordinated to the bank mortgage.

**Quantity survey method of construction** (or reproduction cost evaluation)   Estimating the quantity and quality of each building component, and the cost of the labor to install it. It is the most accurate method of cost estimating, used mainly by contractors.

**Quitclaim deed**   An instrument granting all interest in a property (house) to the grantee (receiver) without a guarantee of title. Often, in a divorce or business partner split, one party gives the other a quitclaim deed. Because a title search was conducted before the couple's house purchase, and the house is in two names, title is not in question (both parties would have to sign for a second mortgage).

**Radiant heating**   Steam, electric, or hot water heating conduits installed in floor, walls, or ceiling of a structure.

**Rafter**   Boards (joists or beams) supporting the roof.

**Rate**   A ratio. In appraisal, the NOI divided by the sales price or value equals the overall capitalization rate. The reciprocal (inverse) is the gross rent multiplier (GRM) for a house. A rental house that sells for $80,000 and whose NOI (income after expenses and vacancy rate) is $4,000 per year has an overall capitalization rate of $4,000 divided by $80,000, which equals .05, or 5 percent. Its GRM is $80,000 divided by $4,000, or 20; 20 times 12 (converted to months) equals 240. Not a very good buy!

**Rate of return**   The rental house's NOI/sum invested in a house, including sales price.

**Ratio**   Quotient; Relation between numerator and denominator. (3 to 4 is 3:4, 3/4, or .75.)

**Real estate**   Refers to land and buildings plus other appurtenances, such as barns, basketball courts, or fences.

**Real estate cycle**   The "boom and bust," up and down movement of real estate prices, as a result of supply and demand economic activity. Often good times elevate prices, bad times depress prices.

**Real property**   Rights, benefits, and interests in the ownership of a real estate parcel. This can include such items as mineral rights, air rights, riparian (water) rights, use (defined by zoning).

**Recapture of purchase capital**   Process by which owner recovers his original investment, usually by mortgage or rental payments and sale price.

**Recapture rate**   The yearly income divided by the original investment.

**Reciprocal**   A number divided into one. Reciprocal of 3 is 1/3; of 8 is 1/8. In appraising, the reciprocal of a rate is a factor, and vice versa. Sometimes used synonymously with inverse. The inverse of 3/7 is 7/3.

**Recording**   The entering of a copy of a legal document, such as a deed, in a government office provided for this purpose. A public record is made for the purpose of constructive notice.

**Regression** A measure of closeness of the relationship of two or more variables.

**Remaining economic life (REL)** Number of years remaining in a house or component of a house. A five-year-old average house with a 50-year life has a 45-year REL. If abused, it may have a 40-year REL.

**Remodeling** Changing the style, structure or plan of a house to correct functional deficiencies; for example, adding a second bathroom to a three-bedroom house, or curing physical deficiencies, such as a leaky roof.

**Repairs** Current expenses to keep up or maintain a property.

**Replacement** Substitution of a new equivalent appurtenance or part of a building for a worn one—a new A/C, for example.

**Replacement cost** The cost of construction of an "equally useful" structure.

**Reproduction cost** Construction or installation cost of an **exact replica.** Usually used on historical sites.

**Residence** Any property used for a dwelling. Legal domicile.

**Residual process** A technique of the income approach. Quantity left over at the end of an appraisal process. If your neighborhood has three vacant lot sales at $25,000 each, and three house sales (similar to your house) at $100,000, you know your lot is worth about $25,000, and by **residual** your house is worth about $75,000.

**Reversion** Return of real estate rights to the grantor.

**Right of way** Usually an easement. One party may have the right of passage or of restricted (utility) usage on another person's property.

**Riparian rights** Referring to the bank of a body of water, as a lake or river. Right to use the water for swimming, business, and so forth.

**Row houses** A series of individual houses with common walls, often facing the same direction. A type of townhouse.

**RTC—Resolution Trust Corporation** The phoenix government agency that arose from the ashes of the Federal Savings and Loan Insurance Corporation (FSLIC) on August 9, 1989. Designed to liquidate the $2 billion to $6 billion in real estate and S&L corporate holdings that are the result of the "Great 1984–88 S&L Debacle." This agency is now under the aegis of the FDIC.

**Sanitary sewer** Human and industrial waste carried via large underground pipes. Excludes rainwater.

**Sash**   Framework holding windowpane(s) in place.

**Scuttle**   Framed opening in ceiling, fitted with a cover, opening to truss roof supports.

**Septic tank**   Sewage depository. Bacterial decomposition takes place, with residue water seeping into surrounding soil.

**Set-back**   Minimum distance from street for building frontline, which zoning regulations dictate.

**Shake**   Wood roof-shingles.

**Shoring**   Temporary supports and bracing used during construction.

**Short-lived items**   Refers to economic life. All items except exterior walls and (if present) concrete foundation of house, which are long-lived.

**Siding**   Finish lumber, aluminum, or other material used on exterior walls.

**Site**   A parcel of improved land, ready to use as homesite, parking site, and so forth.

**Skylight**   A glassed opening in a roof.

**Slope**   The inclination of a surface; deviation from the horizontal; 45 degree slope is a 1:1 slope (1 foot out, 1 foot down; a 22.5 degree slope is 2 feet out, 1 foot down). Angle of repose is steepest slope resisting gravity induced slides.

**Soil obsolescence**   A new phenomenon resulting from soil contamination due to radioactivity, lethal gases such as radon, or hazardous waste. It can be curable or incurable, temporary or permanent. Love Canal area soil, soil near county "Mount Trashmores" with hazardous leachates are obsolescent.

**Special assessment**   Government property tax surcharge for a localized, specialized purpose, such as road swales (shallow curbing), fire hydrants, or lighting.

**Split-level house**   House with two or three levels, usually only two to five feet elevation difference.

**Square foot cost**   Building costs divided by gross living area. Cost of building plus lot divided by gross living area; cost of land divided by land's total square footage.

**Stairway (staircase)**   Flight of steps and landings composing passage from one floor to another.

**Standard deviation**   Statistical measure of extent of absolute dispersion, variability, or scatter in a frequency distribution.

**Straight-line depreciation**   Method of estimating capital recapture. For example, a $90,000 house with a 50 year life and 2 percent straight line depreciates at $1,800 per year.

**Stratified market**   Segmented, urban real estate market; among other segments are commercial, industrial, housing, and agricultural. Housing may be further segmented into rental, single family, condo, and so forth.

**Stringer**   Long, heavy horizontal beam supporting a floor; inclined staircase support.

**Stud**   Vertical, usually two-foot by four-foot board to which wallboards, electrical outlets, and sometimes minor plumbing are affixed (after drilled holes).

**Subordination agreement**   Subordinated party allows another party to have superior claim on an interest in real estate. Second mortgage holder (often seller) or mortgage company is subordinate to first mortgage holder, usually a bank.

**Substitution principle**   A valuation principle; a prudent, typically informed buyer would pay no more for a piece of real estate (subject) than the cost of acquiring a similar property (a comparable)—that is, a buyer will substitute alternatives for subject.

**Subsurface rights**   Right to use and profit from underground portion of a designated parcel. Often refers to tunnel, underground utility construction.

**Sump pump**   Automatic electric pump in a pit in house basement. Used to evacuate water.

**Superadequacy**   Above-average quality or capacity for the area. Prudent purchaser would not pay for such ''luxury'' under current market conditions.

**Surface easement**   Right to use only the surface of the land, as for drainage.

**Survey**   Process of scientifically ascertaining the quantity and location of a parcel, via boundaries, elevation. May include quality of land (soil composition).

**Tangible property**   Touchable. Sensible. Land, buildings, machinery, cash.

**Taxation**   A system for raising revenues.

**Tax base**   For houses, the assessed value. For income taxes, the net taxable income.

**Tax bill**   Proposed tax notice arrives during month 1. After a month of public hearings, final tax bill arrives about month 3.

**Tax deed**   Deed conveying title to property bought at tax sale or auction. Absolute title may or may not be conveyed, depending upon laws of particular state.

**Tax exemption**   Total or partial freedom from tax. Total—religious, government-owned property owners. Partial—veterans, homesteaders.

**Tax lien** (or tax certificate)   Like a high yield local government junk tax bond whose collateral is private property. Every year, county tax collectors take millions of dollars in delinquent real estate taxes and auction them off as receivables. The buyers are willing to accept the lowest interest rate below the delinquent 18 percent penalty. As long as property owners don't pay taxes, these debt instruments accrue interest, generally ranging from 11 percent to 16 percent. However, inner-city property from the Bronx to Boise (literally) is being abandoned and repossessed by the government in lieu of tax payment.

**Tax rate**   Tax/tax rate ratio, usually expressed in tenths of a cent, or mills. The amount of the tax levy, say $30,000, over the total assessed value of the tax district, say, $1 million, which would be 30 mills, or 3 percent.

**Tax roll**   Official list of each taxpayer (TP) subject to property tax.

**Tax sale**   Sale of taxpayer's property for tax delinquency, and failure of taxpayer to redeem property within statutory period.

**Tenant** (lessee)   In general, the renter who lives in the property under a lease.

**Terrace**   Similar to patio; condo terraces are semiroofed; usually house is not.

**Terra cotta**   Hard, kilned, unglazed, molded earthenware used for decoration.

**Tier**   A row or column of items (for example, a tier or column of 1/1 condos, 14 floors high).

**Title**   The composite of all elements that constitute ownership.

**Traffic**   Movement along a path, as a bedroom to kitchen traffic pattern.

**Tuck pointing**   Filling and sealing joints between bricks or stones with a new mortar.

**Underimprovement**   A building or appurtenance that is inadequate to develop the highest and best use of a site, such as a "cheap" house in a good neighborhood.

**Unit cost** (unit price)   If one square foot of a certain type of building costs $40, 1,000 square feet will cost 1,000 times $40, or $40,000.

**Value**   The present worth of future benefits arising out of ownership to typical users or investors. Quantity of one thing (say money) that can be exchanged for another.

**Variance**   Statistical measure of degree and spread among a set of values. Measure of tendency of individual values to vary from the mean value.

**Wainscot**   Wooden lining of an interior wall. Tiled wall area in bathroom or kitchen.

**Wall bearing**   A wall supporting vertical construction, such as a second floor or roof.

**Warranty deed**   A deed granting the purchaser title to the property free and clear of all encumbrances, except those enumerated in the document.

**Wasting assets**   Diminishing assets.

**Waterproofing**   To seal against water or water damage.

**Water rights**   Riparian right, or right to definite or conditional flow of water. Increasingly important in western states.

**Weatherstrip**   Thin strip of metal, rubber, and so forth to fill space between door or window sash and jamb, keeping out air and water.

**Weighted average**   An average in which each component is adjusted by a factor that reflects its relative importance to the whole.

**Wraparound mortgage**   A mortgage subordinate to but inclusive of an existing mortgage or mortgages on a property. Usually a third party refinances by assuming the existing mortgage and obtains (wraps around) a junior mortgage.

**Zoning variance**   Change or variance in the use of a property, unique to the property. Example: 160 Elm Street gets a lifetime variance to keep a boarder in a single-family neighborhood.

# Bibliography

Applied Residential Property Valuation 101, 102, SREA 500+ pp.

Appraising Residential Property, American Institute of Real Estate Appraisers (AIREA), 1988, 442 pp.

Black's Law Dictionary, 5th ed., H. C. Black, West, 1983, 855 pp.

Corpus Juris Secundum, vol. 84.

Ellwood Tables: Real Estate Appraising and Finance, AIREA, 641 pp.

Environmental Audits, University of Florida, TREEO Center, Gainesville, FL 1988.

FNMA Appraisal Guide, MS130A04/88, FNMA, 1988, 68 pp.

Guide to Appraising Residences, H. G. Stebbins, SREA.

Income Property Valuation, W. N. Kinnard, Jr., D.C. Heath, 488 pp.

Professional Guide to Real Estate Development, Dow Jones, 306 pp.

Real Estate Appraisal Terminology, AIREA/SREA, 1985, 304 pp.

Real Estate Finance, W. R. Beaton, Prentice-Hall, 247 pp.

Real Estate Investment, W. R. Beaton, Prentice-Hall, 358 pp.

Real Estate Tax Shelter Desk Book, Institute for Business Planning, Inc.

Real Estate Data, Inc. (REDI), for recent sales, etc.

West's Annotated CAL Codes, Revenue and Tax Code Sec. 402.5.

**Journals**

*American Journal of Economics and Sociology*

*Barron's*

*Illinois Business Review*

*Journal of Real Estate Taxation*

*Medical Economics*
*Property Taxation Journal*
*Real Estate Appraiser and Analyst*
*So You Want to Be a Tax Consultant*
*The Wall Street Journal*

# Index

# NOTES

# NOTES